Applied Photovoice in Criminal Justice

Building on her leading research in creative methodology, in this book Wendy Fitzgibbon explores and illustrates how Photovoice, a participatory, active research tool, can enable new insights and engagement with both marginalised people and those working with them in the criminal justice system. Through the use of research examples from criminal justice settings around Europe, the book explains how to undertake such research and face the ethical and practical challenges presented.

Engaging, accessible and illustrated with original photographs, this book not only presents the theoretical and practical information necessary for researchers, students and practitioners to be able to utilise Photovoice, but demonstrates these with original empirical findings from an international range of projects, including work with probation officers, with female offenders and with the inmates of an open prison.

Written in a clear and direct style, it is essential reading for all those engaged with criminal justice, criminological research methods and visual criminology.

Wendy Fitzgibbon began her career as a probation officer and is now Reader in Criminology at the University of Westminster. She has maintained strong links with the probation service and associated voluntary sector organisations. Her areas of research are Privatisation and Criminal Justice, Risk Management and Visual Criminology.

Criminology in Focus
Series Editor: Sandra Walklate

This series offers a space for a "short format" book series which showcases and puts the spotlight on new research in criminology. We are interested in books that fit the "short-form" model; for example: theoretical think pieces, developments in criminal justice policy, paradigm-shifting innovations in the fields, a compelling case study that would be of interest to an international readership. We would like to attract "big names" as well as up-and-coming scholars; all books should speak and contribute to international criminological debates and conversations.

Applied Photovoice in Criminal Justice

Voices Made Visible

Wendy Fitzgibbon

Routledge
Taylor & Francis Group

LONDON AND NEW YORK

First published 2022
by Routledge
4 Park Square, Milton Park, Abingdon, Oxon OX14 4RN

and by Routledge
605 Third Avenue, New York, NY 10158

Routledge is an imprint of the Taylor & Francis Group, an informa business

© 2022 Wendy Fitzgibbon

The right of Wendy Fitzgibbon to be identified as author of this work has been asserted in accordance with sections 77 and 78 of the Copyright, Designs and Patents Act 1988.

British Library Cataloguing-in-Publication Data
A catalogue record for this book is available from the British Library

Library of Congress Cataloging-in-Publication Data
A catalog record has been requested for this book

ISBN: 978-0-367-86137-7 (hbk)
ISBN: 978-1-03-230035-1 (pbk)
ISBN: 978-1-00-301712-7 (ebk)

DOI: 10.4324/9781003017127

Typeset in Times New Roman
by Newgen Publishing UK

"Accessible, authoritative, and theoretically informed, *Applied Photovoice in Criminal Justice* is a much-needed, practical guide to this increasingly important research technique. Drawing on material from across a range of projects, the text is enlivened with examples demonstrating the critical potential of the method. It is a must buy for students and scholars alike."

Eamonn Carrabine, Professor of Sociology, University Of Essex

"Visual literacy has become as important a research skill as analysing interviews and interpreting statistics. Wendy Fitzgibbon not only explains how to understand images in criminal justice, but equips the reader with new skills and, using international examples, demonstrates how those without 'voice' can co-produce new knowledge through Photovoice."

Anne Worrall, Emerita Professor of Criminology, Keele University

"Participant Action Research by visual means is finally being passionately advocated within criminology. Wendy Fitzgibbon's newest book is a compelling, informative and internationally concerned guide to a cutting-edge research approach. It is necessary reading for anyone interested in doing research within public and visual criminology."

Bettina Paul, Senior Researcher in Criminological Social Research at the Universität Hamburg

"Building on the author's pioneering work in criminological research, this book provides an exploration and overview of Photovoice as a participatory research approach. In the context of an increased emphasis on the importance of co-production within the criminal justice system and in allied fields, this book by Wendy Fitzgibbon provides a timely and important contribution."

Nicola Carr, Associate Professor in Criminology, University of Nottingham

For Two Inspirational Women
Ashleigh Temperley
And
Carolyn Kardia

Contents

Figures

1 Introduction

It is a truism to state that we live in the age of the visual image. Traditionally, text predominated over the visual. Images were described by text, but text was only "illustrated" by images as a sort of optional extra to portray what had already been explained by text.

This dominance of text has been breaking down for some time. Beginning with newspaper photography stretching back to the nineteenth century and then through the growth of film and television the role and ubiquity of the image as a form of communication has steadily increased. Recent years have seen exponential growth in the role of the visual image as a source of information and communication. This has involved not just new forms of image creation, for example, digital photography, but the mass diffusion of the means of image production.

The causes of this are of course profoundly technological—obviously the internet is a major factor. But the internet is as much about text as images. However the production of mountains of text and the consequent overload on people's available time pushes towards the visual image—not just the photograph but also the mind map or the icon as a form of information transmission that is faster than text.

Another aspect of the technological revolution is the progressive cheapening and mass diffusion of the technology of simple digital image creation. The disposable camera, but in particular the smartphone and the tablet combine the means of image production and transmission. A "selfie" taken on a smartphone can be transmitted onwards in a matter of seconds to friends or to wider social media sites. It is estimated that the total number of photographs taken since the invention of photography up until 2011 was around 3.8 trillion. But in 2015 alone, the number of photographs taken was 1 trillion (Kane and Pear 2016).

The effects of the rise of visual culture are the subject of debate and controversy. Critics argue that the rise of image culture has led to a

DOI: 10.4324/9781003017127-1

decline in reading and writing, and some are concerned about a possible dumbing down of thought processes and a reduction in the attention spans, particularly of young people immersed in a culture where the rapidly changing video image is the norm rather than the stability of the text (see e.g. Wilmer et al. 2017). Text itself also becomes subject to a shortening process, as illustrated by the restrictions on the maximum length of a Twitter post.

Early critics of the increasing use of visual image in, for example, advertising focused on the likely capacity of powerful corporations to use films and videos containing subliminal messages as part of mass advertising campaigns (e.g. Packard 1957). The subsequent mass diffusion of personal technology capable of digital production, as with the smartphone, by no means necessarily reduced the power of the advertising industry. As David Buckingham (2009) reported,

> In the field of consumer research, for example, companies have increasingly adopted more ethnographic and "creative" approaches, such as providing participants with disposable cameras, asking them to produce drawings or visual designs, or to make video diaries.
>
> (Buckingham 2009: 634)

The potentially creative self-expression of ordinary people armed with image-producing personal technology becomes absorbed into the media and advertising strategies of powerful corporations. We are also aware of the fact that even where image production and transmission is highly democratised—as with the uploading of personal images to websites—young people in particular can become trapped in a social media world where competitive visual presentations of self become a source of "body image anxiety" stress and depression (Kelly et al. 2018).

But there is another side to the coin, which is where this book starts. The availability of a relatively cheap personal technology of image production—disposable cameras, smartphones and tablets—when utilised by committed social researchers, community organisers, and those concerned to give a voice to the hitherto unheard, *can* become a vehicle to the development of critical ideas, narratives and personal biographies which simply would not be available in a world monopolised by text or the transformation into text of recorded speech. There is a democratic possibility, which in the right conditions can be realised.

Indeed, there are critics who reject the rise of the image as an undermining of independent thinking capacities and see the visual as a process which can go beyond text and is capable of enhancing thinking processes and presenting new ways of understanding phenomena (see

Stephens 1998). Additionally, not only can images potentially encapsulate complex meaning, they can also crucially for the purpose of this method, give voice to people otherwise excluded from textual and coherent verbal accounts. People who lack the textual and verbal resources to describe their feelings or their understanding of what is happening to them can, by starting with visual images, develop new modes of expression.

The first ingredient of our discussion in this book is the capacity of the visual to give a voice where text and speech fail. The second ingredient is the democratic diffusion of this visual capacity through cheap technology. Many media researchers and academics have understood this democratic potential and have sought, as a consequence, to simultaneously democratise and "visualise" (i.e. deploy the image as a bearer of meanings and feelings) the research process.

> Traditionally, only the researchers have operated the cameras; yet in recent years there has been a growing emphasis on the potential of collaborative production, in which participants in research are themselves involved (to a greater or lesser degree) in creating representations of their own experiences.
>
> (Buckingham 2009: 634)

This is precisely where the strategy of Photovoice—using visual images to give a voice, as the name implies—begins. But the understanding of Photovoice as a strategy of democratic, participatory, research—sometimes called "action research"—must also be aware of some of the dangers and pitfalls involved. Thus Buckingham criticises what he identifies as a naive empiricism in simplistic ideas that handing out cameras will enable participants to "tell their own stories" (Buckingham 2009: 635) free from the bias and selectivity of the visual eye of the researcher. That is something we shall be aware of in the chapters that follow, and we shall endeavour to elaborate, through case studies, the meaning of co-participation in which both the researcher and the participant are the authors and interpreters of the visual images which the research project produces.

Despite these dangers, which we hope to acknowledge as the book progresses, the overwhelming advantage of Photovoice is that it responds to the increasing need to find ways of engaging with the marginalised and dispossessed. What needs to be stressed is the simultaneous rise in the importance of the visual image as a form of communication and that of growing social inequality and the increasing marginalisation of disempowerment—economic, political and social—of poor people and poor communities. It is the understanding of this dual process that gives Photovoice its critical edge as a methodology. Photovoice enables the use of the technology of the visual image to give a voice to the poor and marginalised for whom political institutions and verbal/textually articulate elites decreasingly function as representational conduits.

There are broadly two uses of Photovoice as democratic participatory photography. One is its role in the (initial stages of) political mobilisation of marginalised groups. A second, and on which this book concentrates, is the enabling of particular isolated and disempowered groups—such as war veterans, disabled people, probation clients—to give a voice to their feelings and experiences of treatment by larger bureaucratic organisations, whether health authorities or the criminal justice system. The other important dimension is that practitioners within those organisations, who may already believe they know how their clients experience their supervision or support, can learn from these insights and thus develop new policies which respond to this feedback and enhanced knowledge.

It is on this latter use of Photovoice which this book is based. Specifically, the focus is on the use of the technique within the criminal justice system with offenders on probation. This is a group which may already have troubled lives and for whom visual media may provide a mechanism to articulate their actual experiences of probation supervision. This method can also enable probation practitioners to learn what is actually happening to those they supervise and think they understand.

This book uses material from a number of Photovoice action research projects. These were funded by the European Union's (EU's) Cooperation in Science and Technology (COST) programme, which supports projects across the EU member states in a number of diverse areas. These include technology and climate change as well as criminal justice. This COST project was the study of the experience of supervision by offenders on probation.

The aim was to make up for the fact that most research in this area has been on "mass incarceration"—the prison system—rather than the "mass supervision" of those within the community, a far more numerous population under probation supervision. The COST project was thus important in raising the profile of probation, long considered the poor relation of the criminal justice system and with a consequent low visibility.

Probation clients proved a very useful group of people who could take advantage of the use of visual media in Photovoice to articulate how they experienced the actual process of probation supervision, something that has been slipping away in recent years with the decline of therapeutic interventions and the rise of risk management approaches.

The book begins (Chapter 2) by setting Photovoice in two contexts: the wider context of the increasing role of the visual as a theme in criminology at the most general level, and the more specific context of a number of visual techniques—photo-documentation, photo-elicitation—and what is specific about Photovoice as in many respects the most radical of these techniques.

Chapter 3 summarises the main stages in the organisation of a Photovoice project. Obviously there is a great deal of literature and experience on this, some of which we draw on to illustrate how Photovoice is used in a variety of contexts. The chapter then focuses on some of the specific issues arising from the use of Photovoice in work with offenders in the criminal justice system

Subsequent chapters utilise a number of case study reports to illustrate the dynamics and potential of Photovoice. Chapter 4 focuses on work with women offenders and the type of themes arising. This project was supported by the Howard League for Penal Reform. There follow a couple of country studies which were funded by the COST programme. Chapter 5 reports on a project carried out with probation clients in Germany, and Chapter 6 on a study undertaken in Ireland.

We then return to some more general themes. Chapter 7 discusses the use of Photovoice in an educational and training context with students and practitioners working within the criminal justice professions. Finally, Chapter 8 concludes with a theme less well trodden in Photovoice studies—the role of the audience, those who at the end of the day look at and react to the photographs produced by the participants. The theme is that the audience may be important stakeholders in the project and much of its ultimate outcome will depend on how they respond to the work of the participants. This chapter also considers how audience reactions can in themselves provide data, which again provides unique insight into the attitudes and understanding of policymakers, practitioners and the general public.

The production of this book owes a debt to a number of people who were directly involved in the research projects or a major support to the author whilst writing this book. The author wishes to thank Maria Anagnostaki, Kristel Beyens, Lawrence Burke, Anita Dockley, Christine Graebsch, Deirdre Healy, Carolyne Kardia, John Lea, Laura McDavitt, Fergus McNeill, Bettina Paul, Ineke Pruin, Camille Stengel, all involved in the COST Offender Supervision in Europe group and, of course, most importantly of all, the participants/co-researchers who made this book possible.

References

Buckingham, D. (2009) "'Creative' visual methods in media research: possibilities, problems and proposals," *Media, Culture & Society*, 31(4), pp. 633–652. doi: https://doi.org/10.1177/0163443709335280

Kane, G. and Pear, A. (2016) "The rise of visual content online," *MIT Sloan Management Review*, 4 January. Available at: https://sloanreview.mit.edu/article/the-rise-of-visual-content-online/ (Accessed 6 March 2021).

Kelly, Y. et al. (2018) "Social media use and adolescent mental health: findings from the UK Millennium Cohort Study," *eClinicalMedicine*, 6, pp. 59–68. doi: https://doi.org/10.1016/j.eclinm.2018.12.005

Packard, V. (1957) *The Hidden Persuaders*. London: Longmans, Green.

Stephens, M. (1998) *The Rise of the Image, the Fall of the Word*. New York: Oxford University Press.

Wilmer, H.H., Sherman, L.E and Chein, J.M. (2017) "Smartphones and cognition: a review of research exploring the links between mobile technology habits and cognitive functioning," *Frontiers in Psychology*, 8. doi: https://doi.org/10.3389/fpsyg.2017.00605

2   Creative Methods
Placing Photovoice in Context

On 25 May 2020, a public execution took place in broad daylight on the streets of Minneapolis, in the US state of Minnesota. A white police officer, Derek Chauvin, slowly suffocated to death a black man, George Floyd, by kneeling on his neck. The police had been called because Floyd had, it was alleged, attempted to buy cigarettes with a fake $20 bill. The execution took, according to the *New York Times* of 31 May, 8 minutes and 46 seconds to complete. Floyd was heard to utter the words "I can't breathe," a phrase which has become a liturgy for the numerous deaths of African Americans at the hands of violent police officers across the US in recent years. Even when Floyd was lying on the ground motionless, Chauvin's knee remained on his neck.

Deconstructing the Spectacle

How do we know such details? Incredibly, almost the whole incident was filmed on mobile phone by a bystander. The video footage went viral and there followed, all across America, days of protest and rioting, further police violence, hand-wringing by the liberal establishment, right wing attempts to blame the violence on agitators, and threats by the then-US-president, Donald Trump, to call out the regular military onto the streets. Protests also developed across the world as people in many countries grasped the iconic power of the video as a visual indictment of their own policing systems. The power of the visual image in crime and criminal justice could have no more potent and tragic reminder than this.

Both in the representation of the criminal offender and the working of the criminal justice system criminologists have in fact long been aware of the importance of image and spectacle. In the late 1970s, sensitive undergraduates recoiled at Michel Foucault's graphic description of the public torture and dismemberment of the French regicide Damien

DOI: 10.4324/9781003017127-2

in 1757—the last person to be executed in France by such methods (Foucault 1977).

Foucault, together with most historians of the pre-modern criminal justice system, understood the function of the public hanging of the criminal offender as a visual spectacle intended to inspire in the crowd awe at the power and justice of the monarch, his judges and hangmen, and ultimately of God himself in whose name they acted. Of course, in those days the visual demonstration was reserved for the crowd actually present at the hanging. Textual accounts such as ballads and pamphlets conveyed only a fraction of the power of the spectacle itself.

Foucault famously argued that as the focus of punishment shifted from the body of the offender to the Enlightenment-inspired rehabilitation of their soul, so its implementation disappeared from public gaze behind the austere walls of the prison. However this is only partly true. The "spectacle of the scaffold" was to a considerable extent replaced by a new photographic "spectacle" diffused through the modern mass media and which therefore involves not just the executioner and the crowd at the scaffold but the entire population who participate in the production and reproduction of the photographic image of the offender.

The photograph, in other words, is not just the inert representation of its subject but rather itself "a social practice of production [...] [and part of a mass culture which] [...] involves us all in the social practices of spectacular production" (Carney 2010: 18). The spectacle of the scaffold is replaced by the "power of the circulating photograph to stigmatize the body of the criminal in front of a mass audience" (Carney 2010: 21). The growth of photographic reproduction from the original popular illustrated newspaper to the viral video of contemporary social media has continually amplified the role of the image as the producer, rather than simply the recorder, of reality. In the case of the criminal offender, the image involves "not only an indication of policing power in general but also [...] its capacity to brand a detained body with shame" (Carney 2010: 23). If spectacle of the scaffold was the *symbolic* voice of traditional monarchical power speaking through the body of the condemned, the representation of crime in the mass media is the *photographic* voice of the modern state speaking through the digital image of the stigmatised criminal. In recent British criminal history, the iconic images are probably still those of Myra Hindley and Ian Brady, the notorious "Moors murderers" child killers of the mid-1960s.

Critical criminology struggles to deconstruct the traditional criminal justice process as a process of at least partially arbitrary power while seeking the redemption of the criminal as at least partially the victim of circumstances played out through their own personal tragedy. Just as traditional critical criminology sought the deconstruction of the spectacle of the scaffold so modern *visual* criminology seek the deconstruction of the *photographic* voice of the mass crime media. Both are revealed as the legitimation of arbitrary power.

The Image as Voice

Visual criminology as a variant of critical criminology seeks not only to understand how the visual media has continued and reconstructed the modern spectacles of punishment but also aims to return voice to the offender even while acknowledging the harm that they may have inflicted. Its commitment is to "understanding the power of the image in the perpetually mediated worlds of control, crime, harm, resistance and violence in which we exist" (Brown and Carrabine 2019: 194). This task is complex and open-ended. It embraces the study of the visual representations (of crime and punishment) articulated though social media, architecture and space, surveillance, advertising and all the "vast economies of the image" (Brown and Carrabine 2017: 2).

How is voice to be returned to the offender, or the victim of power? Return for a moment to Minneapolis. The viral footage of Floyd's murder was not just the photographic voice of police power. We saw at the same time the democratisation of the moving image in the dramatic power of the bystander and the mobile phone to connect in real time to online social media platforms and thereby transform Floyd's execution into the spectacular indictment of Officer Chauvin and his associates in front of a global audience. The resulting ten or more days of mass protest throughout the US and in many other cities around the world, the political crisis of the US elite, the visual exposure of heavy-handed and arbitrary police response the length and breadth of the country all show the video as counter-power. The development of social media and cheap phone cameras has at least partially wrenched control of the photographic image from the hands of state power and into those of the masses. The image moves from its role as part of the modern spectacle of state power to an equally spectacular role in the provocation of resistance.

Visual criminology forms a part of the emergence of a third stage in the spectacle of judicial power. The first was the pre-industrial spectacle of the scaffold and the public execution graphically (and almost visually!) portrayed by Foucault. The second was the photographic voice of state power when control of the visual image of the criminal was still largely in the hands of the state and the newspaper and media elite. The third, the period in which we now live, is that of the partial democratisation and global diffusion of the image as interplay or *terrain* of contested power. It is against this background, starting from the fact that the photograph provides a "real flesh and blood life experience" (Becker 2002: 11), that *Photovoice* emerges as a tool for the marginalised and powerless to resist the many voices and techniques of the powerful—which of course themselves include the visual—and to articulate their own personal struggles against a power that would dis-member and fragment them.

But Photovoice is more than simply the use of photographs—*our* photographs versus *their* photographs, the visual image of resistance versus the mass media visual compulsion to conform. Traditional radical organisations—trade unions, socialist political parties and organisations—used photographs—in newspapers, posters, party pol-itical broadcasts and so on. These were and are often very moving and powerful images as the long traditions of radical photojournalism demonstrate. But they form for the most part the reinforcement of a narrative sustained by an organisational and political leadership embedded among its supporters through political education, campaigns and local organisations of various types. The photographs *reinforce* the message of the organisation, which was already understood by the mass membership.

A second, more spontaneous variant can be seen in the viral video of the murder of George Floyd. The power of that video lay in the fact that the majority of people watching it knew precisely what was going on because they had seen or heard it countless times before; they had discussed what it meant countless times before. And they had taken to the streets in anger against it countless times before. They did not need a political leadership to tell them what to do or provide a verbal or textual narrative to tell them what the video was about and how to respond to it. They saw it as iconic representation of the police violence they had suffered for generations. They were provoked by the video not only to mass demonstrations but to think through policies to change the nature of police action. One result was the development of a movement for "defunding": for spending less of local and state budgets on the police and more on social services and community development.

Was this collective, large-scale, automatic Photovoice? Not quite. It was less a question of getting people to look at the video and begin to articulate a world view that could lead to action for change than a media event which triggered mass anger and action along the lines of "enough is enough" precisely because African American communities and others too were all too well aware of what the issues were. They had been suffering them for decades. The video did not have the effect of allowing them to formulate what the issue—racist police violence—actually was, but gave them the occasion and the will to mobilise. Photovoice and similar techniques are relevant at a more basic stage: that of enabling communities to formulate what the issues are, to put their diffuse feelings of injustice into a more precise form through the use of photographs and discussion. And in this regard Photovoice is part of a family of photo-techniques for getting people to articulate their views.

Gillian Rose, for example distinguishes between *photo-documentation* and *photo-elicitation*. These are in the main research techniques rather than ways of helping people or provoking political mobilisation. In photo-documentation,

> a researcher takes a carefully planned series of photographs to document and analyse a particular visual phenomenon. Photo-elicitation asks research participants to take photographs which are then discussed in an interview with the researcher; the data generated in this case consists of both the photograph and the interview.
>
> (Rose 2016: 308)

So photo-documentation is "leadership-oriented." It is almost a visual variant of a focus-group technique. For example, a political party could employ researchers to show a series of photographs, carefully taken so as to potentially evoke a particular response by the public. Before it deploys the photographs in its propaganda, the party wants to know whether in fact they do provoke the response envisaged. So it employs the researchers to discuss the photographs and explore the meanings involved. The method is "top-down." The researchers provide the photographs and a list of questions, which the participants then explore. So, retaining the focus on police violence, a political party or other organisation which wants to know which response will meet with most public support might show carefully chosen photographs of police violence and then ask participants to respond. Among the questions which the researchers might ask are: "Do you think this sort of behaviour on the part of police officers is legitimate?" "Do you think that it is typical or exceptional?" "What do you think is the best way of reducing the amount of this sort of behaviour?" and so on.

Photo-elicitation is where the Photovoice movement is mainly situated. It is more bottom-up, democratic. The researcher provides the cameras and the general theme, and the participants go out and take photographs which seem to them to be related to the theme. The theme may be, for example, a general feeling of dissatisfaction with security in the area. Participants will go out and take photographs. Some may, for example, take photographs of rubbish and broken fences, others may portray police officers engaged in various actions, whilst others may take pictures of rough sleepers. The researchers and the participants then *jointly* discuss the photographs and their meaning. The overall diffuse worry about security may then be formulated through the photographs and the discussion to arrive at a list of elements of insecurity in the area, which may well include police aggression, urban poverty and rough sleeping. The photographs may then be "audienced" at a subsequent exhibition and possibly be taken up by a political party which wants to address grievances in the area.

The use of the camera to give a voice to the participants is central to Photovoice. The researcher is no longer the exclusive owner of expert knowledge. The participant is rather a co-researcher and full partici-pator in the knowledge generating process. There is no privileging of the researcher as the legislator of what is important (Chio and Fandt 2007: 486). Although the terms Photovoice and photo-elicitation are often used interchangeably, some see Photovoice as a more democratic variant such that "photovoice offers a critique of photo-elicitation in that it argues that empowering participants necessitates putting them in control of processes of image creation" (Mannay 2016: 23).

Photovoice is much more suited therefore to situations where there is no organisation which already has a policy and wants to find out if it is popular, but rather organisations which want to get people to articu-late their feelings, however diffuse, so that some sort of policy can then be formed to represent those feelings at the political level. The use of the visual image of the photograph is crucial in this process of moving from the diffuse sense of wrong or grievance to an articulate analysis. Reacting to an image is different from reacting to a written text or a speech. The latter are essentially linear processes, while the contempla-tion and discussion of a photograph encourages a much wider range of reactions in different directions and to make connections which might have not been made in responding to a linear text. In their 1975 portrayal of the lives of migrant workers moving within Europe, John Berger and Jean Mohr provide a mixture of photographs and texts with the injunction

> The book consists of images and words. Both should be read in their own terms. Only occasionally is an image used to illustrate the text. The photographs [...] say things which are beyond the reach of words. The pictures in sequence make a statement: a statement

which is equal and comparable to, but different from, that of the text.

(Berger and Mohr 1975/2010: 11)

Visual methods such as interpretation of photographs are inherently democratic. All participants are experts. This can increase the self-confidence of those whose educational and literacy backgrounds restrict their ability to interpret and comment on text (see Rose 2016).

The typical use of Photovoice in its early years was by a community organisation wanting to get people to translate a diffuse sense of grievance into a more articulate set of political changes around which they could mobilise. But the use may also have a very particular and individual function. It may function as a vehicle to help individuals verbalise why they are in the predicaments that they find themselves. This may be a stage in a process that leads to collective community or political mobilisation, or it may be a stage in a journey of individual life change. We can give some examples of both.

Photovoice and Community Action

The classic use of Photovoice is as part of collective mobilisation for social change. The key account is that by Wang and Burris (1997) based on their experience of mobilising women for social change in Yunnan province in China. Photovoice, claimed the authors, "uses the immediacy of the visual image to furnish evidence and to promote an effective, participatory means of sharing expertise and knowledge" (Wang and Burris 1997: 369). The authors quoted a social documentary photographer, Lewis Hine, to the effect that "If I could tell the story in words, I wouldn't need to lug a camera" (Wang and Burris 1997: 372).

Wang and Burris saw Photovoice as a process involving three stages: "selecting (choosing those photographs that most accurately reflect the community's needs and assets); contextualising (telling stories about what the photographs mean); and codifying (identifying those issues, themes, or theories that emerge" (Wang and Burris 1997: 380). Each of these stages is of equal importance. Photovoice is not about replacing narrative with photographs. It is about using the photographs to provoke a narrative, which then leads to proposals for action. The "voice" part of Photovoice was derived from an acronym, "Voicing Our Individual Collective Experience." Key was giving voice to "those whose voice was not heard or present in the policy arena" (Milne and Muir 2020: 5). Wang and Burris gave the example of one of the Yunnan women who photographed a farmer wearily stooping to collect water.

This, together with other photographs of women hauling heavy water buckets and dredging wells, provoked a discussion on access to clean water and how important it was in the lives of the women, and the need for better sanitary conditions. Local administrators were confronted with the photographs and the women's concerns, with the result that the construction of clean water reservoirs moved up the list of local priorities (Wang and Burris 1997: 381–382).

What was therefore key, and what distinguished Photovoice from older methods of "photo novella" in which photographs were used in educational literacy campaigns, was, firstly, the recognition that photography could tap forms of knowledge not yet formulated in narrative and, secondly, the orientation to mobilisation for social change. "This early photovoice ultimately sought social change through dialogue based on the images and narratives of participants which reflected the perception and values of participants" (Mulder and Dull 2014: 1017). The key element of giving a voice to marginalised social groups has been a constant element however it is used. Indeed, both for groups oriented to community-wide social change and for individuals oriented to self-reflection and empowerment, Photovoice has increased in importance.

In fact, Photovoice has been used as a resource for community mobilisation in precisely the area with which we began this chapter—racism and oppression in the US. In the US state of Kentucky in 2015, the motives behind the West Louisville Photovoice project included the fatal police shooting of black teenager Michael Brown in 2014 in Ferguson, Missouri. The ensuing global publicity "gave rise to substantial political will within city government to create and implement strategies to reduce violence and promote social cohesion" (Wendel et al. 2019: 2). This led to funding for a Photovoice project which "enabled local residents to give voice to their lived experience in a public forum, adding their voices to the local conceptualization of issues that need to be addressed" (Wendel et al. 2019: 13). The organisation of the project reflected the origins of Photovoice as bottom-up "action research" and involved a network of community activists and civic groups. Over 40 local participants were drawn from a wide spectrum of the local population. The participants then, over the period of the project, took photographs—using their mobile phones or cheap throwaway cameras—of local scenes which to seemed to them relevant to issues needing addressing. These included institutionalised racism and white supremacy alongside community safety, justice and the combating of a sense of hopelessness about the possibility that conditions could be changed.

Each participant then discussed three or four of their photographs and those of other group members. The aim was to show how the pictures spoke to the experience of both the participants who had taken the photograph and the others, why this experience existed and how it could be channelled into action. The project concluded with a public exhibition of the photographs aimed at interaction and engagement with the wider community as part of a process of political mobilisation for change. It is important to understand that Photovoice does not dispense with either verbal or textual narrative. In the West Louisville project, the researchers

> began with initial coding of text segments from participant narratives, followed by an iterative process of grouping and re-grouping in order to identify emergent themes, accounting for themes identified by each group during its respective discussion. In addition to thematic analysis, facilitators' field notes identified recurring themes that arose from group dialogues and from supplemented participant narratives for accompanying photos.
>
> (Wendel et al. 2019: 5)

The role of the photographs was to provoke reflection and discussion. This was then recorded and classified—by the research team—into key themes for further reflection and articulation by the participants. Photographs, verbal discussions and the production of text were all in a dynamic dialectical relationship as part of the project. In understanding Photovoice as an instrument for political change, it is therefore important to understand precisely what the *photographic image* contributes to the process of mobilisation. Plenty of social movements and political campaigns have been launched and indeed succeeded without the explicit use of Photovoice. If Photovoice is simply the fact that most movements for social change will make use of video and photographs uploaded to social media for distribution to whatever audience is regarded as significant, then it is hardly a specific technique. Rather, it is a simple reflection of the fact that political mobilisation takes place in a world in which the image predominates, as we noted above, as not just the reflection but the production of lived reality. Two examples may help underline the specificity of Photovoice as a form of "action research."

Of course, another way of formulating group opinions is the public meeting model. But people who will attend a public meeting are already aware of an issue and have formulated it even in an elementary way, in their minds. The meeting will generally have been organised by an articulate community group or political party and will reflect a level of political consciousness and coherence which is precisely the aim of techniques like Photovoice to achieve. A community meeting for action might well be the outcome of consciousness-raising activity by organisers using Photovoice among their techniques. But the public meeting itself is not a substitute for the prior organisation, and it is at this level that Photovoice as a form of "action research" is most useful. It operates at a prior preverbal stage when the priority is tackling a sense of hopelessness and confusion about how to formulate this issue in such a way that different sections of the community can synthesise their ideas as a basis for action. This can overcome the fragmentation which otherwise might result in public meetings failing to formulate plans for action because people cannot agree on how to define the issues. The participants create through photographs and their appraisal the very articulate sense of grievances and the possibility of a remedy which can be presented next time an episodic event or a meeting comes around.

The West Louisville project researchers understood the unifying role of the discussions around the photographs and the final exhibition as an

> inclusive process [which] allowed the study to attend to differences in experience and perspective (for example youth compared to older adults), while also recognizing common themes across those diverse experiences that point the community toward possibilities for collective community action.
>
> (Wendel et al. 2019: 3)

But at the same time the project exhibited a certain political naïveté concerning the political and class division which can easily be covered up by the concept of "community." Having celebrated the diversity of participants in the "inclusive process" in their study as drawn from "youth, older adults, LGBTQ people, faith leaders, educators, activists, and two groups of Black men—one specifically comprised of men who had been justice-involved or engaged in illegal activity," they then appear perplexed that

> despite substantial efforts to recruit individuals representing law enforcement, the research team could not overcome officers' reluctance to speak publicly on issues of justice and racial equity. Despite attempts to recruit social service providers and local business owners, scheduling proved prohibitive to their participation.
>
> (Wendel et al. 2019: 4)

To the extent that Photovoice is a tool for community mobilisation, then it is inevitably likely to alienate those representing local or national power elites who are the very targets of community mobilisation.

Indeed, Wang and Burris, working in China, were only too aware of the political context of their project and how this may lead participants to engage in self-censorship from political or cultural motives about what is an appropriate subject for a photograph. Thus the organisers of the Yunnan project "asked women to photograph evidence of conditions and problems they would like to see changed, but they refrained from asking them to focus on the most politically sensitive topics" (Wang and Burris 1997: 374).

The other side of the coin is that the importance of Photovoice as a tool is related to the increased social and political marginalisation of poor communities, the sense of hopelessness to which the West Louisville project referred, and the weakening of other forms of community cohesion embedded in organisations like trade unions, political organisations and ethnic advocacy groups. Indeed a crucial stage in the project is the dissemination of its results, and such organisations may play a crucial role here. Photovoice projects have been criticised for paying insufficient attention to the impact once the project has been completed (Milne and Muir 2020: 7). In the West Louisville project, a local African-American cultural organisation was instrumental in helping to establish the concluding photographic exhibition through which the results of the Photovoice project could be disseminated to a wider audience. This process of "audiencing" is an important component of Photovoice as a practical strategy, and as Linda Liebenberg observed, needs careful planning:

> Most photovoice projects "give voice" by means of community exhibitions. However, this dissemination process is seldom discussed in detail in published reports: How were images exhibited? How were findings reflected in the exhibited images? Who attended the exhibition? How did the audience respond to the shared content? And how has the exhibition informed change?
>
> (Liebenberg 2018: 5–6)

Photovoice as Self-Reflection

Of course, Photovoice can take a non-oppositional orientation more the form of "best practice" dissemination. In this form it is used in community development projects in the global south, sponsored by governments, aid organisations and other NGOs to, for example, overcome community resistance to new forms of economic activity. The UK charity "Photovoice" (<photovoice.org>) "uses ethical photography to promote positive social change" in sponsored projects worldwide. For example, a project in Ghana in 2018 aimed to break down reluctance on the part of young people to enter the construction industry. A similar project in the same country in 2015 was helping farmers increase their business and technical agricultural skills (see: <photovoice.org/constructing-futures/> and <photovoice.org/mypharm/>). The methodology appears to be that a group of participants—already working in the construction industry or, as in the second case, already using new farming methods, take photographs of their activity and then, through "audiencing" by means of photographic exhibitions accompanied by speeches and explanations, aim to break down resistance to innovation. The difference from the type of situations we have been discussing hitherto seems to be that those taking the photographs seem less involved in discovering and exploring their own feelings than communicating the advantages of their situation—through audiencing exhibitions—to wider sections of the community. This might be classified as a form of photo-documentation rather than photo-elicitation.

In other cases Photovoice techniques may be used with particular groups of disadvantaged and marginalised people aiming to overcome their predicaments and develop the self-confidence necessary to initiate self-change or, indeed, simply to survive. So in the UK, for example Photovoice.org is currently or has recently run projects aimed at helping limb-affected military veterans, young victims of sexual trafficking, young people's experience of adoption and support, young people who have been involved in gang violence and knife crime, and similar projects. In all cases the aim of the projects includes both helping people to articulate their feelings and understandings of the world through the activity of taking and discussing photographs and also helping them to "audience" the results of their work to a wider public. So from its original orientation to community mobilisation,

> photovoice has been adapted and evolved, and a considerable amount of researchers and practitioners have sought to make use of photovoice's specific potential to develop insights into the everyday lives and experiences of people sometimes described as "seldom heard," "hard to reach," and "marginalised." This is with the intention of "giving voice" to people and specific communities, challenging prevailing representations, and exploring "hidden" lives.
>
> (Milne and Muir 2020: 2)

It is not surprising that Photovoice is increasing in popularity. A number of general social factors have been at work over the last two or three decades. They include the fragmentation and cultural diversification of the working-class population, growing social inequality and the marginalisation of the poor—ethnic minority communities in particular—and the decline of mass organisations such as trade unions and local branches of political parties which would act as the conduit for grievance articulation by fairly homogeneous working-class populations organised around employment and the workplace. These changes in themselves create an increased space for and a need for forms of community action and mobilisation which, as with the West Louisville project or the examples given by Wang and Burris, help poor communities to start by using their own resources rather than depending on pre-existing organisational and political structures, even though the latter may render some invaluable assistance at the "audiencing" stage.

Of equal importance to the decline of working-class organisation, indeed a part of the same general process, is the decline of the welfare state. In this context the number of people with particular needs or predicaments, not easily absorbed into the general politics of working-class organisation, or indeed into that of community mobilisation, but falling into the category of "seldom heard" and "hard to reach," has increased dramatically.

No more is this so than among those making their way through the criminal justice system as sentenced offenders. During the post–Second World War decades, the welfare state imposed itself on the criminal justice system in the form of a system of *penal welfare* in which "criminal justice became the territory of probation officers, social workers, psychologists, psychiatrists, child-guidance experts, educationalists and social reformers of all kinds" (Garland 2001: 36). In such an environment the sentenced offender was less marginalised and out of sight but was, on the contrary, the subject of considerable intervention. Critics saw such intervention as a repressive and controlling effort to "reconstruct" the offender in accordance with a predetermined model of the good citizen. Nevertheless, the offender was rarely out of sight of professionals prepared to at least go through the motions of listening and helping or, in the mantra of the traditional probation service, to "advise, assist and befriend." The decline of penal welfare in recent decades has left increasing numbers of offenders, including those in the hands of the probation system, with less and less detailed and sympathetic contact, and with continually fewer professionals prepared, and equipped, to listen and help as they attempt to make sense of how they got into the criminal justice system in the first place and their journey through the system towards exit.

One of the key features of Photovoice, as we have noted, is to tap into sources of knowledge which can be revealed in images before they can be voiced in narrative form. Not only are offenders being

deprived of the type of traditional interactions—for example, with probation officers—which would help them develop their own narratives
about their position in the system, but also the new techniques of risk
assessment and management which have swept through the criminal
justice in recent years (Fitzgibbon 2007, 2008) positively undermine
any coherent sense of self and autonomy. The individual offender—
and this is true in other areas such as social work—finds themselves
increasingly described and treated as the outcome of a series of tick-box
assessments. Their likelihood of successful rehabilitation is no longer
assessed on the basis of detailed personal knowledge by a skilled probation officer but is rather the outcome of their performance on a series
of discreet and fragmented actuarial indicators. The statistical likelihood of reoffending is calculated on the basis of statistics regarding
previous offending, previous involvement with drugs, social class and so
on. Offenders are presented with images of themselves over which they
have no control and, more importantly, in which they cannot recognise
themselves or their own capacity for development. The identity of the
offender as individual is deconstructed into that of a "data-vidual" (Aas
2005: 133).

Photovoice is of vital importance in helping the individual offender
to take back their own identity as a coherent human being and make
sense of where they are and what is happening to them. Given that the
type of interpersonal interaction in which a clear narrative might emerge
has been removed, the priority of the self-directed photography in the
initial stages of a Photovoice project emerges as a vital tool for putting the whole back together again through enabling the individual to
restore some sense of identity and narrative through talking about their
photographs and why they took them. This is what we shall explore in
the remainder of this book.

References

Becker, H.S. (2002) "Visual evidence: *A Seventh Man*, the specified generaliza-
tion, and the work of the reader," *Visual Studies*, 17, pp. 3–11.
Berger, J. and Mohr, J. (1975/2010) *A Seventh Man: A Book of Images and
Words about the Experience of Migrant Workers in Europe*. London;
New York: Verso.
Brown, M. and Carrabine, E. (2017) *Routledge International Handbook of
Visual Criminology*. Abingdon, Oxon: Routledge.
Brown, M. and Carrabine, E. (2019) "The critical foundations of visual
criminology: the state, crisis, and the sensory," *Critical Criminology*, 27,
pp. 191–205.

Carney, P. (2010) "Crime, punishment and the force of photographic spectacle," in Hayward, K.J. and Presdee, M. (eds.) *Framing crime: cultural criminology and the image.* Abingdon, Oxon: Routledge, pp. 17–35.

Chio, V.C.M. and Fandt, P.M. (2007) "Photovoice in the diversity classroom: engagement, voice, and the 'Eye/I' of the camera," *Journal of Management Education*, 31, pp. 484–504.

Fitzgibbon, D.W. (2007) "Risk analysis and the new practitioner: Myth or reality?" *Punishment and Society*, 9, pp. 87–97.

Fitzgibbon, W. (2008) "Deconstructing probation: risk and developments in practice," *Journal of Social Work Practice*, 22, pp. 85–101.

Foucault, M. (1977) *Discipline and Punish: The Birth of the Prison.* London: Penguin.

Franko Aas, K. (2005) *Sentencing in the Age of Information: From Faust to Macintosh.* London: Glasshouse Press.

Garland, D. (2001) *The Culture of Control: Crime and Social Order in Contemporary Society.* Oxford: Oxford University Press.

Liebenberg, L. (2018) "Thinking critically about Photovoice: achieving empowerment and social change," *International Journal of Qualitative Methods*, 17, pp. 1–9.

Mannay, D. (2016) *Visual, Narrative and Creative Research Methods: Application, Reflection and Ethics.* London: Routledge.

Milne, E.-J. and Muir, R. (2020) "Photovoice: a critical introduction," in Pauwels, L. and Mannay, D. (eds.) *The Sage handbook of visual research methods.* 2nd edn. London: SAGE, pp. 282–296.

Mulder, C. and Dull, A. (2014) "Facilitating self-reflection: the integration of Photovoice in graduate social work education," *Social Work Education*, 33, pp. 1017–1036.

Rose, G. (2016) *Visual Methodologies: An Introduction to Researching with Visual Materials.* 4th edn. London: SAGE.

Wang, C. and Burris, M.A. (1997) "Photovoice: concept, methodology, and use for participatory needs assessment," *Health Education. Behaviour*, 24, pp. 369–387.

Wendel, M.L. et al. (2019) "Yet we live, strive, and succeed: using Photovoice to understand community members' experiences of justice, safety, hope, and racial equity," *Collaborations: Journal of Community-Based Research Practice*, 2(1), p. 9. doi: https://doi.org/10.33596/coll.23

3 Photovoice in Practice

So what does a Photovoice project actually look like and how is it organised? In the previous chapter we discussed the use of Photovoice in situations ranging from community mobilisation to individual self-clarification. Whatever the context, there are certain key practical and ethical issues in the construction of Photovoice projects. This is the subject matter of this chapter. We shall attempt to outline a step-by-step account of the stages of a Photovoice research project. One set of issues that arises, however, at the outset concerns ethics and democracy. To put it another way, since Photovoice is distinguished (e.g. from photo-documentation and photo-elicitation) by its commitment to a radical democratic approach both in terms of the participants as themselves the photographers and as collective co-interpreters of the meaning of the photographs taken, issues of power are raised. And they are likely to differ a little if the context is community-based mobilisation or individual self-clarification. First, let us outline the basic stages of a Photovoice project and then we can focus in more detail on the respective roles of the researchers and the participants and also on the questions of ethics and power.

Organising the Project

One of the most elaborate descriptions of the "stages" of organising a Photovoice project is provided by Melvin Delgado (2015). He deployed Photovoice as a tool in his ethnographic research on urban youth in the US, and his work is located firmly at the "community mobilisation" end of Photovoice. Building on previous organisational initiatives, Delgado, in his youth research identified nine steps in the development of a Photovoice research project (2015: 103). Some of these are a useful starting point but need to be interpreted and concretised in the context

DOI: 10.4324/9781003017127-3

of each particular project. So the headings are Delgado's but the commentary is the author's.

Pre-project Considerations Including the Creation of a Project Advisory Committee and Preliminary Fieldwork

This is the main preliminary work aimed at the setting up of the infrastructure, which enables the project to go ahead. It includes obvious things like the securing of funding, the establishment of a committee of relevant stakeholders to advise on and generally oversee the direction of the project, decisions as to where in the community the project is to be physically located (Delgado was working in the context of community activism), the clear articulation of the values—political and moral—which are to inspire and guide the project and, finally, its duration.

All these are important and interact—that is to say, have consequences—for each other. The membership of the advisory committee will be an important signal of the political orientation of the project, whether it reflects basic community values. This in turn may have an influence on the willingness of community members to participate. An advisory committee full of police officers is not going to make much headway in persuading young people who are the frequent victims of police violence to take part. Potential participants want to see people with local status and legitimacy. The duration is particularly important given the key role of the participants themselves in Photovoice. A project which was too long could, like many state-led projects, for example, risk demoralisation and a decline in commitment. It is important that participants can look forward to the end result and its publication and dissemination.

Selection of Project Participants and Leadership

The next stage concerns who is precisely going to be involved in the project. Where Photovoice is being used as part of a community mobilisation project, then the question of who are the participants and who is the leadership will obviously be determined by the political dynamics involved. The leadership may, as in the Louisville project discussed in the previous chapter, be community activists and the participants will be drawn from the community of people that the leadership wants to mobilise: for example, young people in the community who share a general sense of grievance which the leadership wants to make more articulate. As in the case of the general advisory committee mentioned above, the representativeness of the leadership will be an important influence on the willingness of people to become participants.

In the case of more closed work, for example, with veterans or offenders on probation, the population of participants will be more closely self-defining—offenders on licence—but at the same time it will be even more important for the leadership of the project to reassure the participants that they—the leadership—are not spies for the penal authorities reporting directly to the latter on the individual attitudes and behaviour of participants. However, there must be transparency concerning when risk of self-harm or risk to others takes precedence over other considerations (that should of course be covered in the information sheet supplied to all participants). Independent legitimacy will thus be very important here also. The organisers and leaders of the project must go out of their way to demonstrate their independence in the eyes of the "captive" supply of potential participants.

The general legitimacy of the project in the eyes of potential participants is a necessary but not sufficient condition for its success. We have to go further and understand the importance of a number of "micro-factors" which can make or break a project—and this applies whether we are talking about community work or getting probation clients to articulate their thoughts.

There will have to be, for example, attention paid to culturally appropriate ways of recruiting participants. Maybe not expecting participants to turn up on a Sunday, or during Ramadan and respecting cultural sensitivities about dress codes. Young people, for example, may best be recruited through their social networks, maybe using youth workers or local women's centres or ethnic community organisations—whatever seems the most effective means of making contact. Participants may need to be screened for suitability. This might be the case where, for example, various forms of extremism had infiltrated a community, or where some potential participants have a known record of disruption and demonstrative anger. These disruptive influences—which may prevent other participants from functioning properly—need to be carefully screened out if possible. Also, it needs to be ensured that those who actually participate have agreed to do so and do not feel under any coercion that may turn them against the project in any way. The obvious way of doing this is the use of consent forms. Along with this is the issue of any payment to be made to participants. Certainly it is very important to avoid any suspicion of "payment by results," that is, that the receipt of payment or reimbursement of expenses is dependent on particular attitudes or photo-interpretations by participants. However, payment of fares, lunch costs and other necessary expenses is essential to enable the activities to take place comfortably and to ensure the participants are fully reimbursed for their costs.

Finally, there are considerations such as the size of the participant groups. There may be several groups, but experience shows that more than eight people is difficult to handle in intense situations where, at the discussion stage, when all participants are discussing sensitive and challenging topics, the experience can be draining. Some participants prefer one-to-one feedback and discussion, which can also work well. Limiting the number of members of the project group safeguards both facilitators and participants and ensures that everyone has the space to explore their images carefully and in a respectful space. Basically, the project leadership, like the advisory committee, needs to be very aware of all these issues. If it is not, it is probably not going to recruit the participants that it really needs to hear.

Training and Ongoing Support Including the Necessary Management and Care of Equipment and Approaches towards Photography

Delgado makes the important point that the training of participants—how to use cameras, elementary photographic issues such as light and focus—must be very careful to avoid "altering the qualities that made them [the participants] attractive as researchers. In other words, to avoid 'adultering' them'" (2015: 117). The spontaneity of the photographs taken by the co-researchers may be undermined if they are paying too much attention to technical rules of photography rather than the images which have symbolic significance to them. Cameras must be allowed to be used playfully so that mistakes and the learning processes—regarding photographic technique—can be part of the Photovoice project itself and its findings. The imposition of constraints on the process of taking photographs becomes a vehicle for the researchers' own preconceptions and stereotypes to be imposed on the participants. It is therefore best, as far as possible, to leave the participants to their own spontaneity and creativity and power in choosing images and how to photograph them even if on occasion this results in a few shots either blank or too dark to process. Sometimes the "mistakes" elicit insightful conversations or result in beautiful images.

Further Issues

These are the important preparatory stages. At the other end of the project there are important issues associated with the dissemination of results. In Photovoice projects aimed at community mobilisation for social change, it is obvious that the organisers, the participants and the audience may be all part of the same community, and the aim of the project is in reality that of one part of the community, the Photovoice participants, galvanising the rest, the audience, into action. Photos and discussion which evoke experiences of police violence and victimisation will, in a poor black community looking for ways to mobilise against police racism, serve the function of immediate communication: what we have photographed is happening to you all. We need to act. The next stage is political organisation.

But in other cases a particular connection between participants and audience cannot be taken for granted, where, for example, the aim of the project is to enable a group of participants who have felt marginalised and excluded from the community itself to clarify their experience of marginality as a stage in getting the community to recognise their problems. In these cases, the relation with the audience has to be thought through very carefully. As Delgado (2015: 120) notes, there may be a potential conflict between the perceptions of the participants and the perceptions of the audience to whom the results of the project will be disseminated. The audience will not necessarily approach the photographs in an exhibition with the same interests and conceptions as the participants out of whose journey of self-discovery the photographs emerged. Delgado quotes an example from Laverick (2010: 86) which shows some of the issues facing the exhibition stage. "Would the inclusion of descriptive accounts of sexual and physical abuse risk a degree of voyeurism on the part of the audience?" Where the participant photographers are precisely a group who have suffered sexual and physical abuse and marginalisation, then it cannot be guaranteed that a public exhibition will not act to further reinforce that marginality by simply confirming the predominant view of the majority that the victims bring adversity on themselves.

So thinking about the potential audience to whom the results of the project are to be disseminated is every bit as important as the selection of the participants themselves. It is a good idea therefore to have in mind a dissemination strategy from the start (indeed this is often required by funders anyway) so that ideas about reports, blogs and exhibitions can be factored into the early stages of the project as well as later when images are selected by participants. Again, as with the issue of technical training, an extreme form of this could be where the organisers try to force the participants into forms of photography narrative and self-reflection which it is decided in advance will be acceptable to the audience. A Photovoice project which aims to simply reinforce existing prejudices and conceptions is not worth undertaking. Indeed, "we must guard against unintended consequences that can create or sustain injustices and power imbalances and must strengthen forces that can promote social transformation to more just society and societal processes" Reed (2005: 87).

Researchers and Participants

Let us look a bit more closely at some aspects of this. As we have said, the researcher is responsible for setting up the project in the first place and providing the cameras and other equipment. The "researcher" may be the representative of a collective entity such as a community group mobilising for social change or of a government organisation—such as the probation service—seeking to develop more imaginative ways to help offenders through their individual journeys.

The researcher is also important in that it is the different type of relationship between researcher and participants which determines the difference between Photovoice as a method and similar methods such as photo-documentation and photo-elicitation. It is worth once again emphasising the difference between these methods and that of Photovoice. In *photo-documentation* the researcher is completely in charge of the structuring and orientation of the whole project. The researcher constructs a series of questions and themes around which the participants take photographs. This "shooting script" (Suchar 1997) means that the participants, although they may go out and take the photographs, are guided by this predetermined structure. Their task is to illustrate an already prepared theme. The mutual discussion between participants and the researcher is in effect a process of getting the participants to explain to the researcher why they interpreted the latter's shooting script in the way they did and how their photographs answered the questions that the researcher had posed. The outcome is more of an education process in which the researcher is, in effect, teaching the participants how to understand and answer the questions posed in the shooting script. The form taken by the interaction between participants and researcher can be a one-to-one interview or a focus group or seminar.

In *photo-elicitation* this hierarchical relationship between the researcher and the participants is retained even though it may be the latter who go out and take the photographs and to that extent become co-researchers. In this method the photographs may come from elsewhere than the participants. They may, for example, be taken from magazines. So elicitation comes close to Photovoice when the participants take the photographs, but it is still not proper Photovoice because the researcher both selects the photographs to be discussed—the participants might have other ideas about which are the most important photographs they have taken—and frames the questions for discussion and guides the discussion.

So photo-elicitation remains ultimately a top-down process. This may have advantages when it is particularly important for the researcher to maintain direction and control of the discussion. For example, Rolbiecki et al. (2019) used photo-elicitation in a study of how medical patients lived with chronic pain. The method involved a private Facebook group jointly managed by a researcher and a patient living with chronic pain, The Facebook group functioned as a place where patients living with chronic pain were asked to share photos that elicited their lived experience with pain. The researchers guided the participants in the discussion of these photos, and the Facebook discussions were analysed using qualitative analysis computer software. With a topic such as the management of chronic pain, it is important perhaps that even where the participants are themselves raising themes and issues, the researchers put clear limits to the scope of the discussion.

In another example from the global south, Elisa Bignante (2010) describes an environmental protection project which used the method to elicit how village communities in northern Tanzania viewed their relationship with the natural environment. The researchers asked questions about the use of natural resources, and the villagers were asked to respond to photographs of different environmental situations and were also provided with cameras to take their own photographs of the type of environmental or agricultural systems, and animal husbandry they found most acceptable.

But there was, interestingly a Photovoice project struggling to emerge within the process of photo-elicitation. That is to say, that although the researchers already had their clear agendas of questions that *they* needed answers to concerning the most effective ways of implementing policies they had already decided on in broad outline, they became aware that the villagers themselves might have, however collaborative they were with the researchers, their own agendas and interests which were not anticipated by, or compatible with the actual research agenda.

> The researchers must constantly strive to strike the right balance between the desire to let informants express themselves freely, being open to unexpectedly interesting insights that arise during the course of the research, and rigour in ensuring research objectives are addressed and discussion is re-directed to the subject of inquiry. However, it is not easy to know when digression might be useful in achieving research goals (or result in improved empathy between researcher and informant) or is simply misleading.
>
> (Bignante 2010: 24)

In contrast, within Photovoice projects these "unexpectedly interesting insights," rather than appearing as diversions from the main issue, become precisely the main issue. This is the key difference. It is not a matter of investigating how already decided (at least in broad outline) policies can be best implemented but allowing the participants to themselves take part in policy formulation. So although in Photovoice projects the researchers will do the coding and extract the narratives from the participants' photographs, it is the attempt to bring out precisely those subjective meanings and narratives which reflect the orientations of the participants that is prioritised rather than trying to find out how an already decided policy should be best implemented. The essence of Photovoice is the participant as a fully respected co-researcher and initiator of themes and concepts.

Even in Photovoice, however, the organisers and their researchers will initiate the general policy area—working out ways of community organising against racism by government and criminal justice agencies, or helping people to develop the self-confidence to talk about the various types of victimisation they have experienced as part of enabling them to live with its consequences. But the difference will be between "how can we tweak our policies and methods to make them more acceptable to participants?" (photo-elicitation) and "what policies do the participants believe will be the solution to the problem?" (Photovoice). Obviously the distinction is a fine one and any given project may best be described as photo-elicitation or Photovoice at different stages depending on the dynamics involved.

To take another example, this time hypothetical: a government-funded local community development project may plan to create new shops and workshops in a particular locality to generate employment together with replanning of parks and open spaces to enhance the quality of community life. The organisers may have worked out plans, hopefully with some initial community consultation. When the plans are nearing finalisation, there will (again, hopefully) be a further round of consultation, and in addition to exhibiting the usual architectural plans, scale models and computer-generated photographs, the organisers may ask local people themselves to take photographs of which existing scenarios and local spaces are most valued or most regarded as eyesores. This would be a straight case of using photo-elicitation as a tool to refine policy implementation. However, once equipped with cameras, the local community participants may go out and take pictures, many of whose themes are completely unanticipated by the organisers—for example, of toxic waste dumps and overpolicing of young people in public spaces. The organisers may find that the participants have come up with a different set of priorities for community development. This is Photovoice, and the development planners may be faced with a choice of either widening their priorities or being publicly seen to ignore community wishes.

Organising the Participants

Once the role of the participants as co-researchers and originators of themes and concepts is recognised, then a key stage in the organisation of the Photovoice project becomes the process of equipping the participants for this proactive role. Both photo-elicitation and Photovoice require that they be instructed in the use of cameras, iPads and smartphones to take visual images. It is not the technology that makes Photovoice different but the totality of all the stages in which the participants emerge as the key definers of themes and concepts. In photo-elicitation they may be asked to go out and take photographs of what a particular policy implementation means to them; in Photovoice the process of taking and discussing their photographs will enable the participants to help the researchers define what the policy should actually be. But in both, the initial stages will involve both a briefing session where the project is explained in detail and instruction in the taking of photographs. At this stage also any restrictions on the scope of the photography must be clearly explained. There may be restrictions, for example, on photographing particular identifiable places or people. This may be especially important in the use of Photovoice in the criminal justice context, which will be the subject of more detailed discussion later in this book. There may also be moral issues about visual representation and these will also be dealt with presently.

After the initial explanation of the project and training in camera use, participants will be given a period of time in which to go out and take photographs. The time period may be quite short. In a project involving offenders on probation in which the author was involved, the participants were given an hour to take ten pictures. In more community mobilisation-oriented projects, the time period may be longer. The acquisition of elementary photography skills—understanding the role of light and shadow, for example—is itself an empowering process and gives the participants access to a whole new world of communication. For this reason alone, discussion is likely to be intense and emotional (Kunimoto 2004).

The next stage is the printing of the photographs and the choice, by the participants, of the most meaningful pictures and the consequent focus-group discussion on emerging themes and concepts. These focus groups enable participants to explore the reasons, emotions and experiences that have guided their chosen images. In this process the freedom of the participants themselves to both control the selection and the number of images, and to choose the captions and the meanings which they attach to the photographs is crucial (Rose 2008). The process is one of critical analysis by the participants of their own images and experiences.

The process of reflecting on the photographs that the co-researcher has chosen can cause the interview to become more intense and emotionally engaging. It enables interviewees to have some distance from their ordinary routines and articulate some of their taken-for-granted practical knowledge, for example, how they negotiate public space or respond to a probation interview. Participants taking photos will be enabled to express their experiences, feelings and their preferences.

This dynamic of critical insight is carried into the coding process whereby the themes and concepts which preoccupy the participants emerge. Looking at and comparing photographs, trying to work out which ones have similar or contrasting messages is a demanding process. The result is a new multilayered understanding of reality, and this is one of the strengths of Photovoice and clearly moves beyond photo-elicitation and generates on the part of the participants new insights into social phenomena which verbal, aural and written data cannot provide (see Bolton, Pole and Mizen, 2001).

Showcasing

The final stage of any Photovoice project is the showcasing of the results through some variety of exhibition. As already mentioned, where Photovoice is used as part of radical community mobilisation for political change, the aim of the exhibition will be hopefully to generalise the experiences of the project participants as representative of the experiences of the community as a whole and so increase the level of political activity. Showcasing in this case is the mechanism of getting others to identify with the participants almost as if they had been participants themselves and so become motivated to support action for change.

But in other contexts the aim is less that of general social change and more that of drawing attention to the particular problems of marginalised groups—such as the mentally disabled, women with health issues, war veterans or probation clients. Now that the group has articulated its problems by means of Photovoice, the aim is to bring them to the attention of those in a position to take further action. These may include welfare or other non-governmental organisations as well as those officially concerned with the issues as a matter of legal responsibility. This orientation to mobilisation and change is part of the "action research" orientation of Photovoice.

But in all varieties of Photovoice, the exhibition stage is much more than simply finding a place to pin up the photographs and invite anyone who wishes to come and look at them. Rather, the exhibition aims to be an effective way of involving these wider audiences in the process of reflection and understanding, so that they will be motivated to act further on the issues (see Andreouh, Skovdal and Campbell 2013). It will also help the actual participants, who will be able to see in concrete terms that they have constructed something, that their work has led to consequences in the form of something that is likely to have an influence on policy or politics. Levy and Weber report on an exhibition as "a source of pride and achievement [...] [for the participants] [...] Some of them dressed up for the event, indicating that it was special to them" (Levy and Weber 2011: 306).

So considerable resources and time need to be devoted to setting up and curating the exhibition. It must convey a message, like a visual essay or story (Kay 2013). Attention must be paid to the sequencing and ordering of the photographs, and indeed which photographs to exhibit, so as to maximise the impact on the audience (see Guillemin and Drew 2010: 185). Delgado (2015: 123) notes a number of positive steps that can be taken to enhance audience effect. The audience can, for example, be invited to respond in writing or answer a short questionnaire. (See Chapter 8 for a more detailed discussion of these issues). Some members of the audience can participate in short interviews, the results of which become a new data source for the project as a whole. Obviously, much depends on the status and organisation of the audience itself. Encouraging community members to become involved in the issues raised by the project requires a different strategy to, say, encouraging a wealthy and powerful charity to finance the further development of the project. It is conceivable that different exhibitions could be mounted for different audiences.

But it is at this stage that any tensions between the organising researchers and the "participants as co-researchers" will most likely to make themselves felt. The basic conflict may be that the photographs which meant the most to the actual participants are not, or are only partially those which the project organisers feel will be most effective in attracting and mobilising outsiders, and so collaborative "co-curation" (Bryce 2013) of the exhibition by the joint work of the Photovoice project organisers and the participants may be placed under stress. Delgado

(2015: 168) emphasises the necessity for the participants to retain control over how their images are displayed and that the organisers and researchers do not allow their attention to the character of the audience to lead them to present images in a way that reinforces negative stereotypes (see also Oleson 2008).

The participants may, for example, have decided that a particular set of photographs have most clearly enabled them to articulate their needs and feelings and so should dominate the exhibition. The organisers, possibly with a wider knowledge of the political dynamics of the community or the institutional politics of welfare organisations and charities, may feel that a different emphasis might be more likely to galvanise wider support or funding. There may also be potential conflict between facilitators/organisers and participants concerning the appropriate audience to invite to the exhibition. Hence caution about the construction of the exhibition is in order:

> Whilst not denying the value and power of imagery produced through such means, one should perhaps question the authorship of the final work (the balance between "facilitator" and "participant") and examine exactly whose thoughts and opinions are being conveyed and whose voice is actually being heard. Such work often suggests that we are being shown a relatively unmediated, authentic "insider" view rather than that of an outside observer (photographer or researcher) and the crucial roles of devising, briefing, editing and presentation (often undertaken by the facilitator) can be minimised, overlooked or even ignored in favour of a focus on the contribution of the participants.
> (Robinson 2011: 131 cited in Delgado 2015: 124)

Power and Ethics

Photovoice is about giving a voice and a new visual language to the unheard. When the unheard—through the Photovoice project—find their voice, it is inevitable that others will react. New voices may produce challenges to established power relations and notions of moral and institutional authority. These may also have reciprocal consequences for the project participants themselves as well as the wider community.

In this context, ethical judgements are inevitable—in particular about the photographs themselves, whether and how they are to be exhibited. We have already noted how these may emerge at the "showcasing stage." One of the problems facing Photovoice as a variety of action research is that there is no particular stage at which the organisers and participants can freeze the dynamic and discuss ethical issues and then implement them. Decisions about which photographs are morally appropriate inevitably crop up precisely in the process of the participants taking them. It is very difficult to say, "only take this type of photograph" when you have just given participants cameras and told them to go out and take photographs that are meaningful in terms of how they understand their lives and situations. Likewise, at the showcasing stage, it is harder to say, "it is best if we don't show these particular photographs," particularly if the participants feel they are really important. It is difficult for the organisers, particularly in a project oriented to community mobilisation, to say, "these photographs will alienate the audience and maybe dry up the supply of potential donors for a continuation of the project." Participants may conclude that the organisers are trying to reimpose the very power relations which the Photovoice project was itself designed to challenge. These issues will arise and will have to be solved "on the fly." The tensions and possible conflicts need to be acknowledged at the outset.

The complexity of the situation is acknowledged by many researchers in the Photovoice arena. Delgado refers to "the need to acknowledge the interrelationship between researchers, participants and community context" (2015: 153). Pink notes the demand that researchers "develop an understanding of the ethical context in which they work a reflexive approach to their own ethical beliefs, and a critical approach to the idea that one ethical code of conduct be hierarchically superior to all others" (2007: 37). All this raises questions about power and norms of ethical behaviour between the key actors in Photovoice: the participants, the researchers and organisers, and the audience. Also, there may be impacts on the wider community.

Participants and Organisers

We have noted the possible conflict between participants and organisers in the context of whose voice predominates at the showcasing stage. Some of this can be minimised if the project is from the outset conceived as a collaborative enquiry with a stress on participatory principles. This, indeed, is what distinguishes Photovoice from simply photo-elicitation and what gives the participants collective inspiration and voice (Liebenberg 2018; Bridges and McGee 2011). Again, this may vary with the character of the participants themselves. In community mobilisation the problem may be less than in work with vulnerable groups such as offenders on probation. In the latter context, stories of severe personal damage may emerge and these may be reflected in the photographs taken. Graham and Kilpatrick's (2010) remarks about Photovoice work with vulnerable children, that "it is the intensity of the stories that emerge that leads to the need for caution when using photographs, or other creative visual methods" (2010: 99), are relevant also in work with groups such as offenders. If, for example, a vulnerable participant takes a photograph of a dead rat because that expresses exactly how they feel they are being treated, it is vital that this is not used by the organisers to further stigmatise the participant or prevent their feelings about their lives being given voice in the first place: "that's a rather gruesome photograph, should we really be using that?" (see also Delgado 2015: 163).

Indeed, such participants may also face violence and intimidation as a normal part of their lives, and when their photographs naturally reflect this, care must be taken to ensure that the result is not further danger. A participant may photograph a location which they associate with victimisation and harm. Organisers must take care that such a photograph, for example at the exhibition stage, cannot be traced back to the participant and so perhaps expose them to further victimisation or threat of physical harm. Ensuring that participation in the project does not further the risk of harm can be a difficult task and "assessment of risk, harm and benefits are far from straightforward. It is not possible to identify all risks that an individual might encounter from participating in research" Wiles (2013: 57).

Participants and Audience

Part of a conflict between participants and organisers in the exhibiting of delicate photographs at the showcasing stage may arise from the latter attempting to anticipate audience reaction and thereby pre-emptively suppressing participant voices. Even if this were desirable, the reaction of the audience is difficult to anticipate and control. Although certain measures can be taken to involve the audience in the project itself (see Chapter 8 for a discussion of "audiencing"), anticipating whether members of an audience drawn from the local public might read some photographs, for example reflecting participant experience of sexual abuse, in a voyeuristic manner is almost impossible. Therefore researchers and exhibition organisers can never be fully in control of the reactions elicited by the exhibitions.

It is not just the organisers but also the participants who may anticipate the audience, particularly if they feel they know who will be attending the showcasing exhibition, and adjust their photography accordingly. Again, this is much less likely in community mobilisation projects than those seeking to help vulnerable, damaged individuals to find a voice. What may be lacking in the latter is a spirit of communal solidarity between the participants—and indeed involving the organisers and some members of the potential audience. The process of selecting the photographs and narratives for the showcasing exhibitions may enhance anxieties about the likely reaction of the audience.

The Wider Community

Many of these issues may extend into the wider community beyond the Photovoice project, its participants and their immediate audience. All sorts of locations and objects, which are potential subjects for photographs, may have associations and meanings far beyond the project itself. Political photo-journalists are, of course, well aware of restrictions on their operations: photographing defence installations or indeed any location which may constitute a possible target for terrorism may attract the attention of the authorities and render the photographer liable to police questioning.

There is an obvious injunction against photographs of identifiable individuals. Also, while it is unlikely that Photovoice participants will find themselves taking photographs of government defence establishments, other objects in public spaces may have political or cultural significance, and their appearance in a showcasing exhibition may have an audience impact quite different from that intended by either the photographer participants or the organisers of a Photovoice project. This could have potentially happened in one of the projects in this book where one participant attempted to take a photograph of the court (as part of his journey), which caused quite a reaction from the police security in the area. This did involve the probation centre manager discussing the project with the officer and also reinforcing the parameters of photographic images in terms of safety and ethics with the participant (see Chapter 6 for a detailed analysis of this project).

In another example, demonstrators in Bristol, in June 2020, tore down the statue of Edward Colston, a prominent seventeenth-century slave trader. The statue, and indeed Colston himself, had for many years been a source of controversy in the city. The demonstration and its identification of the statue as underlining an offensive association of Bristol with the slave trade, was part of the global reaction to the graphic video showing the murder by police of George Floyd, mentioned in the previous chapter. It is easy to imagine that the appearance of the statue in a Photovoice exhibition would incite controversy, and it is not difficult to imagine how it might have featured in a Photovoice project oriented to community mobilisation. Public locations have a moral and political significance which identifies them as possible photographic subjects—in this case perhaps as illustrative of racial discrimination. In other circumstances, for example where a Photovoice participant has been trafficked and sexually abused, a photograph of a brothel in the red-light district of a city will have empowering significance to the participant who took it, but perhaps other consequences well beyond the control of either the participant or the organisers of the project.

Photovoice projects, precisely because they aim to give a voice to the unheard, can turn things upside down.

Work with Offenders

We have made various remarks in the preceding discussion concerning the particular problems of using Photovoice with young offenders on probation. Offenders are often people who have had negative experiences in terms of their educational achievement and their literacy skills (McNeill et al. 2011). For this reason, Photovoice can be a valuable technique in helping them to find a voice, increase their sense of self-esteem and confidence, and share emotions and express feelings about their situation (Palibroda et al. 2009). This is important from the standpoint of their rehabilitation.

There are distinct problems in approaching offenders to become participants in such projects. To some extent in all projects the organisers need to demonstrate that they are not representatives of the very power structure by which the potential participants are oppressed. Thus, the police might encounter great difficulty in persuading young people in deprived urban areas, frequent victims of stop-and-search, to join a police-organised Photovoice project which they would most likely perceive as a thinly disguised intelligence-gathering stunt. In the same way, approaching offenders on probation through the official authorities might have similar consequences. Just as young people in deprived areas might be better recruited to a Photovoice project by community workers, probation clients might more productively be approached through non-statutory, voluntary sector agencies. These women's centres and drugs and alcohol advice centres, despite privatisation and the marginalisation of the voluntary sector in probation (Fitzgibbon and Lea 2020), still play some role with offenders. In fact, in a project in which the author was involved it proved very difficult to arrange access to participants through the statutory agencies even though the operations of some of these, such as halfway houses, may be outsourced to private or voluntary agencies.

38 *Photovoice in Practice*

These issues are not surprising. The whole purpose of Photovoice is to give a voice to the unheard whose needs and feelings are marginalised by the official agencies. This is so irrespective of whether the Photovoice project is organised as part of community mobilisation or the development of individual self-confidence in a penal setting. In a community context, as we saw in the US example discussed in the previous chapter, police and some business groups found it very difficult to engage with the project. This was unsurprising since a major consequence of the mobilisation of hitherto silent voices would be understandably the prioritisation of police racism or discrimination by local employers. The same applies to the institutional setting of offenders on probation. It is highly likely that the finding of a voice will involve a critique of at least some aspects of the structures of power and authority in which the Photovoice participants find themselves. In short, the constraints which official institutions may place on the development of Photovoice projects need to be a subject of constant review. Photographs which confront institutional oppression or a lack of concern with participant problems, must not be institutionally marginalised as "not suitable," particularly at the showcasing stage. Photovoice, as an action-research strategy, is of necessity inherently critical.

References

Andreouh, E., Skovdal, M. and Campbell, C. (2013) "'It made me realise that I am lucky for what I got': British young carers encountering the realities of their African peer," *Journal of Youth Studies*, 16, pp. 1038–1053.

Bignante, E. (2010) *The Use of Photo-Elicitation in Field Research: Exploring Maasai Representations and Use of Natural Resources. Echo*Géo, 11. doi: https://doi.org/10.4000/echogeo.11622

Bolton, A., Pole, C. and Mizen, P. (2001) "Picture this: Researching child workers," *Sociology*, 35, pp. 501–518.

Bridges, D. and McGee, S. (2011) "Collaborative inquiry: Reciprocity and authenticity," in Higgs, J., Titch, A., Horsfall, D. and Bridges, D. (eds.) *Creative spaces for qualitative research: Living research*. Rotterdam: Sense Publishers, pp. 213–222.

Bryce, H. (2013) "Navigating multiple roles as a researcher in a Photovoice project," *Groupwork*, 22, pp. 33–48.

Delgado, M. (2015) *Urban Youth and Photovoice: Visual Ethnography in Action*. Oxford: Oxford University Press.

Fitzgibbon, W. and Lea, J. (2020) *Privatising Justice: The Security Industry, War and Crime Control*. London: Pluto Press.

Graham, A. and Kilpatrick, R. (2010) "Understanding children's educational experiences through image based research" in Jones, J.S. and Watts, S. (eds.) *Ethnography in social science practice*. London: Routledge, pp. 18–32.

Guillemin, M. and Drew, S. (2010) "Questions of process in participant-generated visual methodologies," *Visual Studies*, 25, pp. 175–188.

Kay, L. (2013) "Visual essays: A practice-led journey," *International Journal of Education through Art*, 9, pp. 131–138.

Kunimoto, N. (2004) "Intimate archives: Japanese-Canadian family photography, 1939–1949," *Art History*, 27, pp. 129–155.

Laverick, W. (2010) "Accessing inside: ethical dilemmas and pragmatic compromises" in Jones, J.S. and Watt, S. (eds.) *Ethnography in social science practice*. London: Routledge, pp. 73–88.

Levy, L. and Weber, S. (2011) "Teenmom.ca: A community arts-based new media empowerment project for teenage mothers," *Studies in Art Education*, 52, pp. 292–309.

Liebenberg, L. (2018) "Thinking critically about Photovoice: Achieving empowerment and social change," *International Journal of Qualitative Methods*, 17(1). doi: https://doi.org/10.1177/1609406918757631

McNeill, F., Anderson, K., Colvin, S., Overy, K., Sparks, R. and Tett, L. (2011) "Inspiring desistance? Arts projects and 'what works?'" *Justitiele Verkenningen*, 37(5), pp. 80–101.

Oleson, V.L. (2008) "Feminist qualitative research in the millennium's first decade: developments, challenge, prospects," in Denzin, N.K. and Lincoln, Y.S. (eds.) *Landscape of qualitative research*. London: SAGE, pp. 262–304.

Palibroda, B., Krieg, B., Murdock, L. and Havelock, J. (2009) *A Practical Guide to Photovoice: Sharing Pictures, Telling Stories and Changing Communities*. Winnipeg: The Prairie Women's Health Centre of Excellence.

Reed, B. (2005) "Theorizing in community practice: Essential tools for building community, promoting social justice, and implementing social change" in Weil, M. (ed.) *The handbook of community practice*. London: SAGE, pp. 84–102.

Robinson, A. (2011) "Giving voice and taking pictures: participatory documentation and visual research," *People Place Policy Online*, 5, pp. 115–134.

Rolbiecki, A.J., Teti, M., Crenshaw, B., LeMaster, J.W., Ordway, J. and Mehr, D.R. (2019) "Exploring lived experiences of chronic pain through photo-elicitation and social networking," *Pain Medicine*, 20, pp. 1202–1211.

Rose, G. (2008) "Using photographs as illustrations in human geography," *Journal of Geography in Higher Education*, 32(1), pp. 151–160. www.tandfonline.com/doi/full/10.1080/03098260601082230

Suchar, C.S. (1997) "Grounding visual sociology research in shooting scripts," *Qualitative Sociology*, 20, pp. 33–55.

Wiles, R. (2013) *What Are Qualitative Research Ethics?* London: Bloomsbury Academics.

4 Working with Women

It is often forgotten that far more people are under probation supervision than are in prison.

> Even in the world-leader in mass incarceration, the number of people subject to probation or parole far exceeds the number imprisoned; of the 6,741,400 people under some form of penal control at year end 2015 in the USA, 4,650,900 were being supervised in the community.
>
> (Kaeble and Glaze, 2016 cited in McNeill 2019: 208)

When we consider the situation in England and Wales, statistics from the Ministry of Justice show that in those two countries, 230,578 people were under probation service supervision, while the prison population in September 2021 averaged 78,756. Probation also imposes substantial limitations on supervisees' behaviour and choices, giving probation officers enormous power and discretion (Phelps 2017). Yet criminologists, legal scholars and other social scientists have focused very much on populations subject to "mass incarceration" rather than the greater population subject to "mass supervision."

The voices of women offenders under probation supervision are—as those of women in prison—often unheard (Belknap 2020, Birkett 2013). They are perhaps doubly marginalised in terms of voice, both as women and as offenders in the hands of the criminal justice system. This chapter considers Photovoice as an effective way of enabling these women to communicate their experiences. The aim of the projects discussed here was to enable women to generate their own photographs and thereby convey the problems they experience while under supervision and also their aspirations for the future. As a consequence, Photovoice is highlighted as a very useful method for criminological research—an

DOI: 10.4324/9781003017127-4

area of social science research that often deals with powerless and marginalised social groups.

Traditional methods of research with female offenders are mainly based on interviews and group work. These are costly techniques, which often replicate the authoritarian dynamics that further suppress women's voices. This alienation hinders the process of rehabilitation and therefore makes little contribution not only to the lives of the offenders themselves but also to public safety. It is hard to get people involved and to experience any sense of empowerment when they feel marginalised and oppressed by powerful prison and probation regimes which are continually watching them and are "in their face."

Photovoice has proved to be a powerful new model of working with women, giving them a sense of empowerment and personal trans-formation through their own self-generated photographs which, once taken and made real through discussion and mutual validation, cannot easily be annihilated by institutional oppression, however "therapeutic" its organisers and administrators may consider it to be. To the extent that probation—and we are talking about England and Wales—has departed from its older traditions of "advise, assist and befriend" in the relations between practitioner and client and moved in the direction of surveillance, monitoring and tick-box risk assessment of client behaviour (Fitzgibbon 2011), then the potential of Photovoice to estab-lish a more self-affirming "counterculture" among clients is all the more important. Photovoice has already been proven to work with those with mental health problems and those who are socially isolated (Fitzgibbon, Graebsch and McNeil 2017, Fitzgibbon and Stengel 2018), to improve communication skills and self-esteem. These are essential tools for rehabilitation and social reintegration. Photovoice also stresses the shared experience which enables participants to empathise and identify with one another and their victims.

Setting up the Projects

The participants who were involved in these projects which are the sub-ject of this chapter study were volunteers in two distinct groups. The first were ten women, from Alana House Women's Centre in Southern England. This centre provides support, advice and specialist offender-based programmes to both women on supervision and other marginalised women who have often served prison or probation sentences. This was part of a wider project called "Supervisible" under the auspices of the COST (European Cooperation in Science and Technology) Offender Supervision in Europe Group founded in 2014. At the end of this COST project there was an exhibition in Brussels to showcase its achievements. The second group involved eight women from the same women's centre in a funded project called the "Enrich Project," organised by the Thames Valley Police, Reading Borough Council and IRIS.

The visually based action research method of Photovoice offered these women new ways of expressing their feelings. They took photographs and then met in focus groups to reflect upon and explore the reasons, emotions and experiences that had guided their chosen images. They were facilitated in this process by an artist experienced in group work. They then wrote accompanying captions that described the meanings behind their images.

As mentioned in Chapter 3, when dealing with vulnerable people in an institutional setting, it is of the utmost importance to guarantee that participants feel free from coercion or threat of sanctions from supervisors if they decline to participate. We recognised that participants might feel greater freedom of choice if approached via non-statutory agencies such as women's centres. We found that this method seemed to work best when there is an ongoing positive relationship with the gate-keeping agency. This was the case with the positive responses from women regularly attending the women's centre.

Participants were provided with either a disposable (group 1) or a digital disposable camera (group 2) and given information on how to use it. Then they were enabled to take pictures that expressed their perspective on, views about and feelings around supervision, and their lives. The groups met for six sessions over a period of 12 weeks. The photographs were then printed fortnightly and returned to the participants, who chose the images that were most meaningful to them and provided them with a title or caption if they chose to. Participants were involved in group discussions (with all the women who took part in their group), in which the pictures acted as catalysts for the discussion. All the sessions were recorded and transcribed.

The first two sessions of both projects were open ended and allowed the women to freely play with the cameras and interact with each other, building a community where they felt safe and supported to be creative and share experiences. The second two weeks involved going out with participants into the community and engaging with their ideas and discussing the photographs during their creation as well as the results. The final two-week sessions were focused around the selection and planning of the exhibition. At the end, the selection of photographs that emerged from the projects was shown in two public exhibitions hosted by Alana House. The participants' permission and involvement in the selection and in hanging the exhibition was a key part of the process.

By setting tasks and getting the producers of the photographs to interpret the meanings of their images, as well as those of the rest of the group, an intense and transformative group dynamic was enabled. The art therapist and researcher also participated in these discussions to allow for a collaborative interpretative process.

Both the printing and distribution of printed photographs and the recording and transcribing of the focus-group discussions they provoked, were important in stimulating further insight and reflection. Preserving the quality of the images and prints is important in demonstrating respect for the participants' work, as Rose (2011: 250) has argued. Participants also need time and opportunity to reflect on their work and to think of suitable captions and descriptions of the thoughts and feelings represented in or evoked by the photographs. This was facilitated by working with an artist who had experience of photographic art and of working with groups; the artist helped not only in providing advice on taking the photographs but also in supporting safe, nurturing and respectful group discussions. We found that being in small groups of three or four worked best. Larger groups took longer and constrained time for and therefore depth of discussion of the photographs; they could also be emotionally intense and quite draining.

Data analysis raised a range of complex challenges. Analysing visual data—perhaps especially for researchers accustomed to text—is difficult. First, we had to consider whether to start with the images themselves or with the discussions of them. In an important sense, the focus groups were a form of co-analysis of the images; one which began with and privileged each photographer's meaning-making regarding their work, but which also allowed for other participants (fellow supervisees, artists and researchers) to see other things—and to offer other "readings" of the images. With hindsight and with reference to Carrabine's (2014) discussion of the interpretation of images, we can see therefore that both in the focus-group dialogue and in our own analyses, several forms of interpretation were involved. At different times we focused on the objects and forms in the images themselves, at others we focused on their representational meanings—both as offered by their "authors" and as interpreted by their "readers."

Interpreting the Photographs

The focus-group discussions in which the photographs were interpreted was the core of the Photovoice project. The recording of these sessions then provided the textual analysis from which participants could make further reflections to concretise the themes that had emerged. The participants viewed and reacted to each other's photographs and so there gradually emerged themes around which the photographs could be clustered. In this chapter the author has made a selection of photographs which were part of the larger portfolio of images showcased in the public photograph exhibitions. These discussions included viewing and commenting on each other's visual data, the participants' social contexts, and the analytic implications of the projects. The common themes, which emerged from both of the projects, were: surveillance and control, judgement and representation, rubbish and waste, help and support.

Findings from the Supervisible Project (Group 1)

Surveillance and Control

Figure 4.1, from the Supervisible project, was taken by Jenny, a participant on probation supervision. It is a close-up of a human eye (the participant's eye). The image was titled "Sobriety," and it conveys a

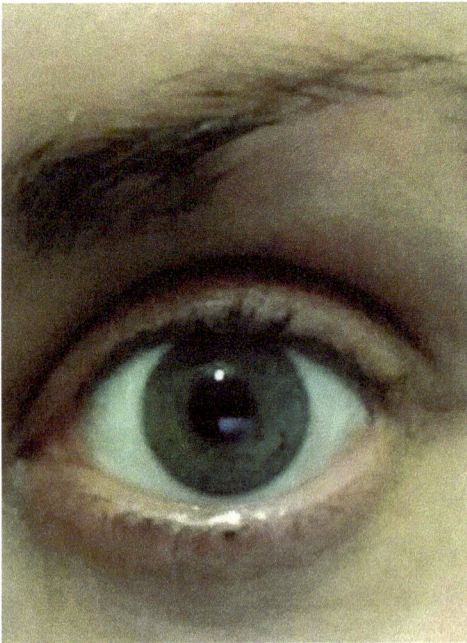

Figure 4.1 Sobriety by Jenny

strong sense of the pains of community punishment. The "all-seeing eye" represents not just the surveillance and control by the probation officer of the client during the periods of active supervision but much more generally it reflects the pervasive nature of punishment in the community.

Jenny, who took the photograph, had a history of alcohol problems but was abstaining during the project, and the photograph of a healthy, clear eye free of jaundice and bloodshot veins symbolised her successful new healthy lifestyle. At the same time, the image serves as a metaphor of how the lives of participants under probation supervision are exposed to others who have power over them in the form of the courts, probation officers, social workers and the police. This image, and indeed several of the other photographs taken during the Supervisible project echoed the theme of how participants under supervision experienced their lives being halted. Their "real life" felt suspended during and sometimes after supervision.

The sense of being subject to a panoptical all-seeing gaze (Foucault 1977, Cohen 1985) wherever the participants sought refuge was never far away. Jenny and many of the other participants were continually conscious of needing to present their behaviour in a certain way, of being exposed and monitored while their very existence was being assessed as "deviant" or failing to conform to the gendered norm for women.

While Figure 4.1 draws on popular motifs in the context of the penal system, the image contrasts with common descriptions of what supervision or social work means within the community. Many of the women's photographs and discussions during the Supervisible project revealed that their interaction was depicted as exposing, as the stark eye suggests. Participants explained how even when the relationship with the supervisor or formal support worker was positive, the association merely served to mitigate the pains of being compelled or constrained to obey authority. However, as Jenny reflected during the focus group, the constraint and monitoring of supervision had enabled her to access the support she required to stop drinking alcohol, which had improved her health.

One of the most common themes to emerge from both the Supervisible and the Enrich projects was "constraint" and "control." This emerged in images and discussions centred on limited freedom, on living under surveillance and regimes of control, on the constant perception of being watched or supervised, and on the barriers that this sense of surveillance imposed on living a full and "normal" life. Indeed, for some of the women in both research projects, the fear of being incarcerated or involved with the police was ever present.

Judgement and Representation

Judgement, labelling and stigmatisation were particular and common themes in the images taken by Supervisible participants. Figure 4.2 was taken by Betty, a participant on probation supervision. Betty was reflecting on her criminal justice journey and her picture is of a painting featuring four different types of women's shoes. The shoes are almost eccentrically individual with respect to various styles and designed for different purposes. She commented that the image was "about the whole judgement—you shouldn't—you don't know a man until you've walked a mile in his shoes."

She was pointing to the stereotypical nature of any criminalising judgement which assigned characteristics and traits based on one aspect of a person's life or appearance. She referred to "man" and "his" shoes, although obviously she was considering her experience which mirrors attitudes regarding gendered experiences of criminal justice being predominately male. This process has become standardised via

Figure 4.2 You Don't Know a Man until You've Walked a Mile in His Shoes
by Betty

technologies, which deconstruct offenders into characteristics that are then scored for risk assessment and resource allocation purposes (Fitzgibbon 2007, 2008). This in itself was viewed as unjust, ultimately a failure to represent the whole person accurately. As Katja Franko Aas (2005) argues, the criminalised individual is deconstructed into a series of data or observable traits which serve to make a "data-vidual," that then operates to displace the context of the person's life. Ideas of representation and judgement were seen by the women to reinforce this lack of contextual understanding.

Figure 4.2 was one of a collection of images in the Supervisible project that presented the themes of representation and judgement. Sally, another research participant, claimed that being on probation means "you are being someone you are not" or "being seen as someone you are not." However, other participants saw probation as also involving taking their masks off—a process which can ease the burden of misrepresentation. As participant Mandy stated, "it was quite a relief when someone actually said 'It's all right, we know what's going on and you don't have to pretend anymore, [who] you are.'" Desistance studies and the resultant literature which has focused on strength-based approaches, has constantly illustrated the importance of genuine communication and acceptance (Maruna et al. 2004, Burnett and McNeill 2005, Fitzgibbon 2007). Figure 4.2 and other visual data on judgement highlight the importance of the research participants' personal relationships with their probation officer. The probation officer's ability to see the real person and their complex life—the exact opposite of deconstruction and stereotyping—was spoken about as key for participants to overcome the negative aspects of monitoring while under supervision.

Rubbish and Waste

Figure 4.3 was taken by Rebecca, a participant from the women's centre. It had no title. Many of the photographs taken by women in both research projects depicted images of litter, rubbish, bins, discarded newspapers, ashtrays with cigarette butts, empty alcohol cans and bottles, and discarded syringes. Participants discussed how the idea of debris either represented their lives or a particular situation or aspect of their lives. Participants who focused their photographs on this theme commonly spoke of feeling like rubbish or shit, feeling all used up and having a sense that their lives were rubbish and that they were worthless. Rebecca took a photo of a blue bag of rubbish that was tiny and hidden under a stairway. She explained, "I was trying to get the rubbish of my life, like the bag, here, this. Everything else is clean and I'm the rubbish

Figure 4.3 Untitled by Rebecca

and I was trying to get that in this one [...] There's clean and there's that rubbish, and I'm that [...] Before probation, yeah, really did [feel like that]!"

Societal judgements portraying "deviant" women as abnormal can become internalised by the women themselves with a consequent self-stigmatisation and deterioration of self-esteem and self-worth (Heidensohn et al. 1985, Measham 2002). Rebecca, for example, had suffered long-term mental health problems which exacerbated her complex material problems and led her to focus on her own failings rather than being able to build on her strengths. Rebecca's participation in the Supervisible Photovoice project enhanced her self-confidence to become more engaged in other support groups including a photography group.

Help and Support

Although the participants in the Supervisible project were women in vulnerable life situations, a selection of photographs highlighted the positive experiences of receiving support and advice and accessing a safe space. The help and support gave rise to a strong sense that the women were resilient, were moving forward and were making positive

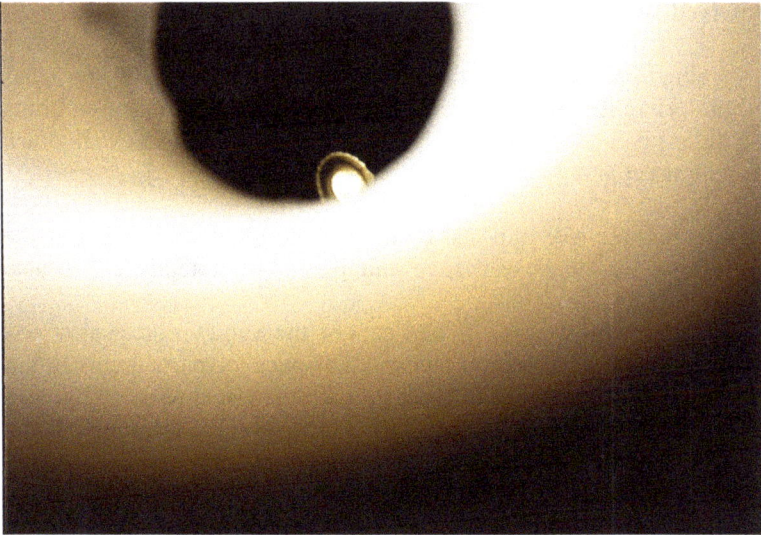

Figure 4.4 Light at the End of the Tunnel by Sophie

changes to their lives with support and encouragement from their probation officers or their key workers in the women's centre.

Figure 4.4, entitled "Light at the end of the tunnel," was taken by Sophie, a participant on probation supervision. Describing the image, Sophie said, "I quite like the way that it sort of just peeks out, rather than being there and whatever else. It's sort of quite muddling through, it seems quite far away there, which is actually how it felt." Sophie demonstrated her awareness of the challenges ahead. Yet despite this, she recognised that positive changes in her life were possible with adequate support. Her conceptual perspective, evident in her image, constructed by using her hand to form a tunnel peering towards the light, indicates her hopes for the future. Yet she placed the light amongst darkness as her quote indicates she is aware of the challenges (darkness) she has to go through to make the light central.

Nevertheless, support was not always easily received by the co-producers of the images. The women often felt that assistance was accompanied by pressures which made them feel infantilised and that were experienced as overwhelming and constraining. The participants were aware of the dual role of supervision: that it aimed to help but that supervisors were also there to constrain and to monitor. Melanie observed how

> going to probation and talking about the way you ought to react as a woman isn't real life. You'd like it to be and at some point hopefully subconsciously it will be but realistically you don't walk down the street and go oh I mustn't react in this way or [...]

She accepts the role imposed by the probation supervisor but at the same time sees it as restrictive and perhaps not realistic (see also Trotter 2015).

One of the most engaging elements of the Supervisible project was how the Photovoice method facilitated a space for participants to tap into their latent creativity, not just through the visual research but also to link their experiences to their future goals and life directions. Jenny encapsulated the desired achievements of many women who participated in this research project. She explained how the services offered at the women's centre encouraged her to try "to be more creative, you know, actually doing something as opposed to just talking about it [...] It just really cheers me up." Since participating in the Supervisible project, Jenny has presented her photographs at the Brussels exhibition and spoken to an audience of over 90 people. Later she was accepted on a fine arts degree course based on her portfolio of creative work. Other participants in this project engaged in art classes locally, prompted by the encouragement and support of the women's centre targeting women on supervision.

These various images and themes are only a selection of the photographic data that was produced from the Supervisible project. They show that, although the process of support and advice provided to women could be helpful and promote recovery or desistance, this engagement was often also experienced as painful and intrusive. Through the themes of judgement, surveillance and control, the photographic data and discussions revealed the pervasive and invasive nature of women's experiences of the criminal justice system and the women's centres they attended.

During the Supervisible project, one woman (Ellen) took a picture of a couch with clock faces printed on cushions. The sofa was in the women's day centre she attended, and Ellen spoke of having spent much time waiting there for meetings or for transport to other meetings and services. But she also spoke of waiting for her life to move on, to start again. She named the picture "Borrowed Time."

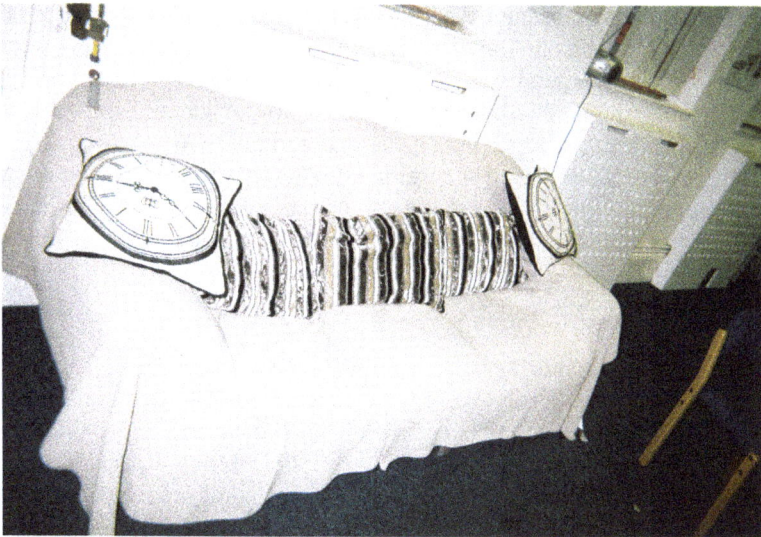

Figure 4.5 Borrowed Time by Ellen

Many participants identified time as a major preoccupation when considering supervision. There were numerous images of clocks or watches in various forms and contexts. These conveyed a strong sense of supervisees "doing time" in a similar manner to those imprisoned. Again, like imprisonment, supervision was experienced as producing a strong sense of suspended time, wasted time or lost time. It was a journey that had to be travelled, and in that process, time sometimes became distorted and confused.

Another woman (Susan) from the women's centre, in a discussion prompted by comparing Ellen's picture with one of her own, reported that she believed she was fighting her own chaos, attempting to order her time (and thus her life) but having little autonomy or ability to do this:

> "I definitely think subconsciously I'm always fighting that chaotic, you know, yes it's regimented and I've got to be there at 11 o'clock and I've got to stay there till 1 o'clock and it's every week and in the meantime I've got to do X, Y and Z on Tuesday and Friday and whatever else but there is definitely a whirlwind in amongst all of that."

(Susan)

The participants—the producers of these images—were often surprised at their ability to create imaginative, original and powerful photographs. The sense of collaboration amongst all the participants (supervisees, artists and researchers) was apparent throughout the process. For all participants, the method allowed an exploration of identity and experience, and the stress on respecting the photographer's intended meaning (even if not to the exclusion of other interpretations) has helped to prevent total appropriation by the researchers of the meaning of [informants'] accounts (Holliday 2004: 62 cited in Fitzgibbon et al. 2017: 317).

Setting Up the Exhibition

Research participants were closely involved with the creation of the photo exhibitions that showcased a selection of the photographic data. With the permission of the participants, the Supervisible project images were displayed in three exhibitions. The first exhibition was held at the Alana House Women's Centre in southern England, the second exhibition was in Brussels, and a third was hosted in Glasgow. The first exhibition was attended by participants, their families, practitioners and local policymakers, and politicians. The second exhibition was held to celebrate and showcase the achievements of the COST research network and the Supervisible project not just in England but also in Scotland and Germany (see Chapter 5 for details of the German project). One of the research participants and the Women's Centre manager were also invited and flown to Brussels where they gave a presentation discussing their experiences of the research study and their own narratives. The exhibition was visited by the general public, politicians and commission staff as well as participants of the COST network and their colleagues. The Glasgow exhibition involved participants and their families as well as professionals and the general public.

Participants also sometimes expressed their astonishment and excitement that their images could elicit deep and insightful discussions as well as very visceral reactions. These reactions now extend beyond those involved in the research itself. These public exhibitions allowed others to engage with the images and the emotions and experiences that they conveyed through lively discussion and thought-provoking feedback. The exhibitions represent an intriguing interface between visual criminology and public criminology (Loader and Sparks 2011).

Reflections on the Supervisible Exhibition

Public engagement via the Alana House exhibition was very positive and incredibly insightful. Although small in number, due to limited invitations, those who attended were really impressed by the quality and variety of the photographs. This was gauged not only by verbal feedback to the facilitators and organisers but also through the comments gathered in the image feedback sheets. No captions were provided, yet the comments show how the discussions and meanings the women wanted to convey were heard and reflected upon by the audience.

Examples of the comments are listed below:

"[CCTV] Camera's are watching"
"Beauty in Ugliness"
"Art and Nature coming together"
"Sanctuary"
"Reflected calm"
"Sprouting beauty"
"Being watched—safety or intrusion?"
"Rainbow of refuse and recycling"
"Restoring the past"
"Modern sculpture for a modern town"
"A tiny light in the darkness"
"The terror of losing your freedom"
"Friendship"
"Odd one not fitting in"
"Home, comfort, routine"
"Fragmented"
"Life is not always light"
"Stop and think"
"Standing out in the crowd-isolated"
"Seen through the windows-not always what it seems"
"Broken but can be repaired"

The Enrich Project

The second project, called the Enrich project, was run in an identical manner to the first project, but the participants had more complex needs and had committed more serious offences. To demonstrate the success of this programme, a few of the women who were involved will be discussed anonymously (pseudonym used only) as case studies to illustrate their progress over just six sessions of engagement.

Sam was a long-term heroine user who had been street homeless for many years. She was particularly hard to engage with via traditional methods. However, she LOVED the project, it became central to her life over the weeks, and she contributed positively and showed a high level of awareness to the needs of others in the group. She arrived early

Figure 4.6 Untitled by Sam

for each session and planned her images carefully and skilfully. For example, she was very proud of a few of her images (see Figure 4.6).

The workers at Alana House noticed how her interaction with other women in the centre improved as did her personal care and appearance, so much so that on the day of the exhibition, she spoke to the public and professionals present and was evidently rightly proud of her achievement. Her key worker is now continuing to use photography as the main method of working with Sam in the future. Sam also asked the artist and the researcher if she could be part of any future programme. Sam said to her key worker, "This is the first time I've been excited about something in years." And others at Alana House said, "She's so excited about this photography project. She lit up!"

Toni was one of the women who had served a long prison sentence and attended the programme whilst living in supported hostel accommodation. She was articulate and engaged, again fully immersing herself in the project and demonstrating an ability to produce powerful and meaningful images which reflected her experiences and her hopes for the future. She spoke very poetically about the alienation and harsh experiences she had had in prison, and the fact that the project was

Figure 4.7 Chaos and Calm by women on the Enrich Project

enabling her to find a voice. Her images conveyed the sense of margin-alisation and surveillance she experienced on her release. Photographs of prohibitive signs, CCTV cameras in greys and blacks and security gates predominated Toni's views of her world. The harshness and sym-bolism of some of her images reflected her sense of feeling constrained and monitored even though the project allowed her individual creativity and confidence to improve. What was particularly touching was Toni developed, designed, drew and managed the group's production of the front cover/poster image for the exhibition. This comprised a collage of some cuttings from the photographs that the women donated from their copies to the project creating an inclusive and representative picture. The women all assisted in this process with Toni's guidance, and the researchers just observed.

Again, the project gave her confidence so that during the last few weeks she started to speak about further education and creative writing as well as arts projects. Once again, she thanked the facilitators very much for their input. She also invited her partner and friend to the exhibition and proudly showed her photographs to them. Toni told others she felt the project was "amazing!"

Monica, another long-term prisoner released and now living in her own flat, approached the group with enthusiasm and a high level of confidence. In fact, at first she appeared to dominate the session, but through the boundaries and exercises within the group, she learnt to support and encourage others, becoming, over the weeks, more empathic and able to allow others to shine and speak out. Her initial manipulations were contained and then her abilities in art were encouraged. She played a very positive role in the planning and organising of the exhibition, leading others to clear the spaces needed to hang the work and again being extremely proud of the overall results, not just her own work. Her images reflected on her ability to notice difference and value colour. She would take domestic shots of balconies with colourful flags or plants, bins that were different colours and sizes. Her eye to see shapes and colour in everyday spaces and objects enabled others to view their surroundings in a more positive light.

Alice was an extremely nervous and underconfident participant initially, feeling very unsure of her ability and potential contribution to the group. However, she managed to find a voice with the encouragement of the other women and went on to produce some challenging images. These reflected her problems with relationships and also memories of happier times when she felt more comfortable and confident. It was evident that Alice felt able to articulate her difficulties and problems with the other women in the group. Their quiet praise and care allowed her to continue her attendance and get involved with other creative groups such as the craft group. Not only did she do this but she encouraged others to join her. Alice said she has moved from feeling "nervous and uncomfortable," to "excited and relaxed about meeting new people within the group."

The project was highly successful with a total of five women who really fully engaged throughout the process. Even though three of the women who started, for different reasons could not continue, their images and their experiences would have been positive. One committed a violent offence and was remanded in custody; one had childcare issues, which prevented her ongoing attendance; and one woman was physically ill and so unable to attend some of the sessions. Interestingly, when discussing the final exhibition, all the women decided that an example of these three women's work should be showcased, demonstrating their partial contributions. The women were also sent copies of their photographs to recognise their contributions.

The support worker reflecting on the project said,

> Photovoice has been an empowering project for the women, that has directly impacted on women's confidence. We have seen direct

positive impact on areas such as improved self-care and hygiene due to increased confidence, interest in photography as an employability skill and reduction in anxiety. The course has given the women a sense of feeling important, recognised and listened to. They have conveyed their awe at knowing they are the subject of an exhibition which is open to the public.

The five women who contributed to the programme decided that they wanted to summarise their experiences with the following statement. I think this is the best way to end this section on the Enrich Project.

Alana House brought us together, the camera helped us talk and as we opened the shutter we opened our creativity, imagination and communication. To find calm in the chaos.

(The Enrich Project members)

Conclusion

The research derived from the two projects outlined in this chapter has shown that Photovoice is an effective and forceful means of enlightening the public, relevant practitioners and policymakers on the complex realities of people involved in rehabilitation supervision, whether on probation or on post-custody licence.

Since research participants are the photographers in the Photovoice projects, they ultimately have ownership of the images they produced. However, the author of this book has reproduced their images in various media, including public presentations, exhibitions and journal articles with their permission. Ethical and legal safeguarding was ensured in order to protect research participants' image ownership. For the first author's Supervisible project, all the research participants signed consent forms about the use of their photographs for exhibitions, articles and other outputs, but they retained their ownership if the image was to be used for other purposes or was commercially used or successful. The women were keen for their pictures to be viewed and discussed by a wider audience and fully understood the safeguards in terms of identity and ownership. This was also done with the Enrich project and the women agreed that their photographs could be reproduced using a pseudonym.

The methodological strength of Photovoice is that participants hold the power to take photographs of whatever they choose, and these images ultimately guide the generation of materials and analysis of the Photovoice research. The author found that their respective research projects facilitated space for participants to be empowered as co-producers through the data generation and knowledge creation processes, as well as through the public photo exhibitions. While the author enthusiastically endorses the potential of Photovoice for criminological research, this endorsement comes with a warning that this is not an utopian methodology that removes all inherent power inequalities in research, nor can it promise social change. As with other forms of qualitative and participatory research, Photovoice should be used with ethical care and active researcher reflexivity (Pink 2007). Furthermore, the concept of participant empowerment through Photovoice should be realistically framed within the structural and material conditions that might disempower participants in their lives. However positive the immediacy of Photovoice may be, the overarching sense of distress, powerlessness and destruction revealed through the participants' pictures heralds the need for structural and political change, which can sustain permanent transformation in their lives. Photovoice research facilitates space for contradictory interpretations to coexist within one image, and through this process can reveal and challenge inherent power inequalities.

References

Belknap, J. (2020) *The Invisible Woman: Gender, Crime, and Justice.* London: SAGE.

Birkett, G. (2013) "'Transforming rehabilitation' for women? A view from the courts," *British Journal of Community Justice*, 11, pp. 149–153.

Burnett, R. and McNeill, F. (2005) "The place of the officer-offender relationship in assisting offenders to desist from crime," *Probation Journal*, 52, pp. 221–242.

Carrabine, E. (2014) "Seeing things: Violence, voyeurism and the camera," *Theoretical Criminology*, 18, pp. 134–158.

Cohen, S. (1985) *Visions of Social Control.* Cambridge: Polity Press.

Fitzgibbon, D.W. (2008) "Deconstructing probation: Risk and developments in practice," *British Journal of Social Work Practice*, 22(1), pp. 85–101.

Fitzgibbon, D.W. (2007) "Risk analysis and the new practitioner: Myth or reality?" *Punishment and Society*, 9, pp. 87–97.

Fitzgibbon, W. (2011) *Probation and social work on trial: Violent offenders and child abusers.* Basingstoke: Palgrave Macmillan.

Fitzgibbon, W., Graebsch, C. and McNeill, F. (2017) "Pervasive punishment," in Carrabine, E. and Brown, M. (eds) *Routledge international handbook of visual criminology*. London: Routledge, pp. 305–319.

Fitzgibbon, W. and Stengel, C.M. (2018) "Women's voices made visible: Photovoice in visual criminology," *Punishment and Society*, 20(4), pp. 411–431.

Foucault, M. (1977) *Discipline and Punish: The Birth of the Prison.* London: Allen Lane.

Franko Aas, K. (2005) *Sentencing in the Age of Information: From Faust to Macintosh.* London: Glasshouse Press.

Heidensohn, F., Silvestri, M. and Campling, J. (1985) *Women and Crime.* London: Macmillan.

Holliday, R. (2004) "Reflecting the self" in Knowles, C. and Sweetman, J. (eds.) *Picturing the social landscape: Visual methodologies and the sociological imagination.* London: Routledge, pp. 49–64.

Loader, I. and Sparks, R. (2011) *Public Criminology?* London: Routledge.

Maruna, S., Porter, L. and Carvalho, I. (2004) "The Liverpool Desistance Study and probation practice: Opening the dialogue," *Probation Journal*, 51, pp. 221–232.

McNeill, F. (2019) "Mass supervision, misrecognition and the 'Malopticon,'" *Punishment and Society*, 21, pp. 207–230.

Measham, F. (2002) "'Doing gender'—'Doing drugs': Conceptualising the gendering of drugs cultures," *Contemporary Drug Problems*, 29(2), pp. 335–373.

Phelps, M.S. (2017) "Mass probation: Toward a more robust theory of state variation in punishment," *Punishment and Society*, 19, pp. 53–73.

Pink, S. (2007) *Doing Visual Ethnography: Images, Media and Representation in Research*, 2nd ed. London: Sage.

Rose, G. (2011) *Visual Methodologies: An Introduction to Researching with Visual Materials.* London: Sage.

Trotter, C. (2015) *Working with Involuntary Clients: A Guide to Practice.* Abingdon: Routledge.

5 Using Photovoice in the German Criminal Justice System

This chapter analyses a Photovoice project undertaken in Germany with people under community supervision at three sites (a halfway house, a resettlement and legal advice centre and an open prison). The contributors took photographs focused on the impact of community supervision, or in the case of the inmates their current/previous experience of the criminal justice system. This then led to focus-group discussions regarding their chosen images, motives and reflections on their lives with the researchers and their fellow participants. This chapter will analyse the research and evaluate not only the results of the project but will raise some questions about the efficacy of the approach and some of the challenges that can arise during such a project.

In Europe, generally while most social scientists have focused on the growth of "mass incarceration," post-imprisonment probation has in fact achieved the dimensions of "mass supervision" (McNeill 2013, McNeill and Beyens 2016). Mass supervision has attracted much less attention from researchers and the media than mass incarceration despite taking place outside the gates and walls of prison (Phelps 2017).

As supervision is often viewed as an alternative to custody and not a sentence in its own right, it has often been neglected (Graebsch and Burkhardt 2015), or seen as a less intrusive or burdensome sentence than custody (Morris and Tonry 1990). However a more recent study in Romania exposed the "pains of probation" supervision from interviews undertaken with probationers (Durnescu 2011).

In Germany, the main form of probation is "supervision of conduct" (*Führungsaufsicht*), which is

> one of the measures taken to reform the offender and protect the public. It is imposed when a sentence committing to a mental hospital or a facility of custodial addiction treatment is suspended

DOI: 10.4324/9781003017127-5

or when continuing accommodation there is suspended, when an incapacitation order or its execution is suspended, or when the court expressly requires it for particular crimes. The most frequent case in practice is supervision of conduct following the full serving of a prison sentence of at least two years, in case of sexual offences one year. The offender is then subject to the control and assistance of the supervisory agency and the probation officer. Supervision of contact can also be linked to instructions. The officer supervising the conduct monitors the behaviour of the offender and compliance with any instructions.

(Jehle 2015: 46)

The number of people under "supervision of conduct" steadily increased from 24,818 in 2008 to 36,706 in 2014. The number of people instructed to maintain contact with a probation officer rose from 27,401 in 1963 to 182,715 in 2011 for the Western Federal States of Germany (Jehle 2015). There is little statistical data regarding the new Federal States of Germany added after the reunification completed in 1990. Thus, many of those under supervision remain statistically invisible.

As in other jurisdictions, young people in Germany experiencing supervision have often had negative experiences of education and have limited literacy skills (Tjettmers and Henning 2016), which can of course inhibit their confidence and ability to verbally articulate experiences and feelings. It is also likely that they have negative experiences of being interviewed either as research participants or under criminal investigation. In this sense they are ideal subjects for Photovoice as an innovative vehicle enabling them to increase their self-confidence and develop new communication skills.

Setting up the Project

The project comprised four Photovoice sessions involving a total of 12 participants distributed over three locations: an NGO legal advice centre and an open prison in Bremen, and a halfway house for released prisoners in Hagen. In the latter location, two groups were organised: one with the residents on probation and one with two staff members who wanted to use the technique to reflect on their own perceptions of their clients' feelings.

An innovative aspect of the research was to choose interview partners and places that were closely connected to the supervising institutions but not part of the supervisory system in themselves. There was an important reason for this. In Germany, the little research that has previously taken place concerning how clients experience probation, has always been dominated by the probation service itself rather than by independent researchers (Graebsch, Von Borstel and Burkhardt 2014). Thus, probation clients have usually been asked, and indeed selected, by the probation officers themselves to take part in research, and interviews have usually taken place in probation offices and with a predominant use of questionnaires collated and returned to the researchers by the probation officers themselves. Unsurprisingly, the results of studies assessing the helpfulness of probation to clients have tended to be rather positive (Beiker 1982, Cornel 2000). As far as the probation clients are concerned, this situation makes research attempting to evaluate the probation experience simply another aspect of the actual probation experience itself. The research is conducted *within* the power relations (between probation officer and client) that it is attempting to evaluate (Graebsch, Von Borstel and Burkhardt 2014).

It is in an attempt to move away from the methodological problems of this type of research situation that Photovoice can play such an important role. The first step was in fact to undertake the research somewhere other than the probation office. The project under discussion here took place, as noted above, in places such as houses for released prisoners and NGOs working with former and current drug users as well as within a more conventional settling of an open prison. Alongside this location of the focus groups/interviews was the novel approach that they took. Questionnaire-based interviews are too text oriented for people who are often without qualifications and sometimes illiterate, and commonly have a history of unsatisfactory experiences in communicating with and within institutions that strongly rely on textual messages (Tjettmers and Henning 2016). This includes educational as well as criminal justice institutions.

Photovoice, as the antithesis to this, was able to capture the enthusiasm of participants and to enable trust between researchers and the probation clients to be established in a more direct and immediate manner than would have been possible with verbal and textual-based research methods such as questionnaires or semi-structured interviews. Verbal descriptions of experiences were important; however, they were elicited not in response to questionnaires but through the clients describing their responses to the photographs they themselves had taken. These individuals had been on the receiving end of verbal interviews and interrogations by police officers and judges, and understood that how they responded may have material implications for their lives—the nature of the charges against them, the length of the sentence and so on. Individuals in such situations naturally develop techniques for responding to and surviving such interviews. By contrast, the free use of the camera and the freedom to respond to their own visual images without any sense that a particular response might put them at a disadvantage became therefore a liberating experience. They could begin to articulate how they really felt rather than having to "deal with" the demands of authority figures and institutions.

Photovoice is a technique that fulfils the requirements of Participant Action Research in that it provides an approach which allows participants to delve into their experiences and perceptions whilst also enabling them through their photographs/exhibitions, to communicate their views to the public and not to be passive subjects of media or academic observations. By participating in a public discourse concerning their experiences of being supervised, the project aimed to empower participants to express their emotions and opinions. The public often are aware of the existence of (sexual) offenders, but rarely is their situation whilst under supervision in the community realised. These offenders are usually just ignored or characterised as monsters or useless. This project wanted to make the participants acknowledged members of society with voices that were recognised and respected. Later in this chapter we will return to critically reflect on this assumption and these aims.

Setting up the project had therefore some clear aims, which were accomplished in a fairly straightforward way both organisationally and technically. The participants (offenders under current or previous probation supervision) were handed a disposable, digital camera and asked to take photographs of their life under the supervision of the criminal justice system for between half to one hour. They were able to walk and choose images freely, and even those in the open prison managed to find access to outdoor space as well as indoor areas in order to compose their images.

The artist involved in the project and the researchers gave the group a brief introduction to the task, and the artist explained the possibilities of using the camera creatively and avoiding identifiable images such as people or places. An interpreter was used, but many of the participants could understand some English. However everything was translated to ensure everybody could participate equally in drawing out common themes and issues.

Once the participants returned to the research meeting, they were offered lunch, self-selected from a pre-ordered menu. This successfully bridged the time until their photos were available to be projected onto the wall of the room. After this had been done, all the participants were asked to discuss their photos collectively. The focus group reflected on their experiences of supervision by the criminal justice system and their lives in general. The photo groups were moderated by the artist and the discussion was translated for the British researcher and the British artist, neither of whom spoke German. The photo group session was recorded and transcribed by the German colleagues for later use. Most of the verbal contributions were in German. Thus the interpretations given by the participants/co-researchers were translated. This proved difficult, especially when trying to decipher the recorded voices and everyday colloquial language. The researchers attempted to be true to the character of what was said to make it easier for English readers. Nonetheless, in a process like this, it is not possible to translate everything without losing and unintentionally changing parts of the content and authenticity.

Interpreting the Photographs

The images and the group discussions were a highly effective method of enabling participants to share their experiences, their difficulties and their aspirations. The artist and researchers were able to quickly build an intimate and trustful atmosphere where participants could honestly talk about their journey through the criminal justice system and their feelings about the effectiveness or otherwise of their supervision, particularly in relation to their future lives beyond the criminal justice system. The staff who participated also revealed a high degree of insight into the situations and emotions faced by their clients. In order to illustrate this, we include a couple of the powerful images they created. The key themes that emerged from the German project were those of time, judgement and waste.

Time

The participants expressed a conviction that their time was seen as less precious or less important than that of those who supervised them. The workers or probation officers were perceived as having a purpose, so their time was precious and was to be respected. The concomitant sense of lack of respect for supervisee's time was clearly demonstrated. One participant (Stefan) discussed his arrival at the probation service after a long journey on the bus (his photograph was of the bus stop). On arrival he had no one to receive him and therefore nobody to talk to but an anonymous telephone in the waiting area; the meeting with the probation officer took place only after approximately a one hour wait in the empty reception area. With experiences like this in mind, one of the focus groups agreed that probation officers often behave as if they and their clients lived in different time zones, with the time of the officers being more valuable than the time of those under probation.

Probation is also shown as illustrating a similar characteristic to "doing time," an expression used to convey the time constraints during imprisonment. Although probation cannot be accused of extreme factual time consumption in the same direct way (i.e. a sentence of three years' loss of liberty), the time on probation supervision does not just equate to the time in front of the probation officer; rather, it involves travelling sometimes quite long distances, and it involves prohibitive conditions regarding work, contact with family and the freedom to do certain activities. As Durnescu (2011) demonstrated during his research in Romania, this continuous feeling of being in supervised time, extends the full length of the probation sentence and reinforces the "pains of probation." A sense of participants' time being devalued, suspended or lost highlighted this and was closely linked to another theme common to all three sites: judgement.

Judgement

The more negative connotations of being compelled to be first and foremost an offender under penal control were reflected in a picture (from the NGO group) presenting a bare-bosomed sphinx-like statute. Karen,

Figure 5.1 Steadfast by Karen

the woman who took this image, said that life under probation feels like being "laid bare but clinging on with claws to remain steadfast." The Sphinx had large and strong claws that rooted her to the plinth.

> *Well, this is, if you are under probation and things like that, then you often feel laid bare. Sometimes like being caught or whatever. [...] Strong claws you must have to pull through. Yes, this is to be steadfast. To [...] that there is no way around that one has to remain steadfast. Must.*

(Karen)

These and other images and discussions revealed and emphasised the importance of the personal relationship with the probation officer. Figure 5.2 below was taken by a man (who for the purposes of the research called himself Vivaldi). He was under a "supervision of conduct" order, a special form of (intensive) supervision after release from prison in Germany (for more detail, see Graebsch and Burkhardt 2015).

Uncaptioned by "Vivaldi"

Figure 5.2 Uncaptioned by Vivaldi

At first sight, this picture seems to fit very well with the official purposes of supervision (for example, supporting people to reduce reoffending) and possibly also with the role perception that many probation officers hold for themselves. But from a methodological perspective, the importance of the focus-group discussions became clear in that it allowed us to hear and heed what Vivaldi meant this image to convey. He associated the woman on the traffic sign with "Lady Justice" and himself with the child that is tied to her determinative hand and not allowed free movement or independent thinking. It might not come as a surprise that conviction itself is often perceived as judgement and sometimes as unfair in its disregard for an individual's motivations and circumstances. However, in the German penal system, the execution or implementation of the sanction is usually conceptualised quite differently. Although including the aspect of control, the implementation of the sanction is formally focused on the rehabilitation or resocialisation of the supervisee (Morgenstern 2015). This image, by contrast to this formal legal understanding of the purposes of implementation of the sentence, presents the supposedly helping hand as a representation of infantilising guardianship and incapacitation.

This picture was one of seven taken by Vivaldi, who now lives in the halfway house in Germany after a period of long-term imprisonment. The others images show his life under supervision as a cul-de-sac, as shoes positioned in a circle so as to appear to be walking, never going anywhere, as a clock standing still at 0:00 and as steps down into a cellar (the last image representing a hardly translatable German phrase for hiding one's feelings from everybody).

In these and other images, a lack of trust towards the probation service was often coupled with significant personal needs and yearning for recognition in the context of lives that had been difficult ever since childhood (represented, for example, in images of backpacks and sacks which are heavy to bear); and where long-standing difficulties have been compounded by the continuing trauma of imprisonment (after release).

Stephan presented a photo of his shoes, taken from above looking downwards (see Figure 5.3). With the support of a social worker in the halfway house he had regained some self-confidence and access to spiritual support. He was definite in stating that he could not have received this kind of support from the probation officer: *"He would be the last one I talked to about this. And I have told him this. Because I am not obliged to, and there is no law that can force me to do so."* He explained further by sharing two images, both showing a chest of drawers, the second picture with the lowest drawer being open. He referred to the German term

Schubladendenken (literally: drawer thinking), a compartmentalised and stereotyped way of thinking that might be translated as "pigeonholing":

> *Each time I am seeing my probation officer—they have these predefined questionnaires, these ones they use. [...] And I am, for instance, I am in the drawer [figurative for: category] "without social contacts," "without work."*

(Vivaldi)

He illustrated this by the example of his probation officer's reaction to the information that he had lost his job:

> *He didn't ask me how I felt in this moment without work. All he was concerned about was that when [it] all goes wrong for me that I could ricochet [meaning figuratively: reoffend]. [...] Another stabilising factor has disappeared.*

(Vivaldi)

Describing judgement and categorisation by the probation service as pigeonholing illustrates the importance of the debate about the so-called risk orientation of probation, which is currently being promoted within Germany. With reference to the experience of England and Wales, where risk assessment has become the dominant philosophy, this approach is promoted to recalibrate the aim of probation towards prevention of relapse and concentration on risk evaluations, while rehabilitation as an aim in itself is denied (Klug and Schaitl 2012). This research study, even though very small in scale, revealed how at least some of the supervisees may be well aware of these "tick-box-approaches" used by the probation service, which may lead to them closing up and denying the trust that is an essential precondition for supporting a process of desistance but also for an accurate risk analysis to be undertaken (see Fitzgibbon 2008).

Waste

The final theme that repeatedly occurred in the focus groups was that of waste. However, this could be seen as a cleansing process as well as one symbolising a sense of worthlessness and "being all used up"(See Fitzgibbon et al. 2017). Probation support only infrequently appears to emphasise the enormous longing for a new beginning in contrast to a dominant feeling of worthlessness which exists, indicating that supervisees rarely feel able to be open to new self-perceptions and positive future

Figure 5.3 Untitled by Stephan

perspectives. The picture above conveys the sense of hopelessness and shame experienced by one of the participants in the project.

> *Stephan: Yes, this photo is for example—walking head down, isn't it [...] After prison.*
> *I didn't like myself anymore. Yes, I also lost self-confidence. What I see most are my feet.*

Rather, probation in this study was repeatedly represented as a comprehensive restriction of autonomy that continues the experience of imprisonment, which goes far beyond specific instructions etc. One of the photographs taken was that of a dog behind a fence, and that was seen as a symbol of how the participants felt whilst on probation in the community. The probation service can obviously be vital and supportive in individual cases, depending on the approach that is utilised and the personal relationship that is established. Predominantly, however, this role, where it was performed at all, was seen by independent organisations as social work "done to" individuals, thus reinforcing their sense of worthlessness and lack of agency.

Figure 5.4 Being All Used Up by Freddy

This sense of being all used up and lacking any future was symbolised by Freddy, who described himself as being all used up like this ashtray of cigarette stubs. He then when on to relate his experiences of being a heroin addict and losing friends, his partner and his health. He was quite traumatised by these powerful reminiscences and as a result, he had an hour-long conversation with the art therapist at the end of this group session to ensure he was feeling more supported and calm before he left the building. This example demonstrated to all involved in the project the importance of identifying and being ready to offer support from a person qualified in group work and able to provide professional advice and listening.

As has been demonstrated in other parts of the book (Chapters 4 and 6, for example), Photovoice exposes raw and very intense feelings and therefore works best within a nurturing and supportive environment. The reactions from Freddy indicate that Photovoice is not a panacea for problems nor does it ameliorate the difficulties and trauma that have been experienced through long-term interaction with the criminal justice system.

Figure 5.5 The Wall by Dennis

Other participants' images indicated a sense of the heavy burdens of the past. Photographs of backpacks, sacks, waste bags and the very powerful image (Figure 5.5) of a wall (symbolising the participant)—that prevented the earth from tumbling down the slope onto them—represent the overbearing weight on the supervisees' shoulders.

> *And the wall. It's a lot of pressure on it. Yeah. The wall that's me, and the pressure comes from the top. The justice.*
>
> (Dennis)

Probation supervision was discussed in relation to this, being constantly under construction or the need to clear away the debris of the past or to rebuild using the materials of the past to secure a new future. The pressure was immense (there were also a few pictures of fire hydrants from a few participants), but these images had a rather more positive aspect than the "condemnation script" depicted by images such as Freddy's ashtray or Stephan's feet (Maruna 2001). According to the findings of desistance research, the exit from a life of crime often succeeds when those affected can write a new story or script about their life in which the past in all its aspects, including their crime(s) and punishment, is understood as meaningful because it is a process which has prepared the way to a "good life" (Maruna 2001).

Photovoice has often been deployed as an *ideal and quick fix* method, yet this naive assumption deserves closer scrutiny.

Photovoice: A Means of Empowerment or Further Reinforcement of Negative Norms?

Photovoice can be grouped into the research methods labelled Participatory Action Research, which primarily aims to empower participants and enable them to tell their stories, thereby gaining agency and a political or social voice which can lead to change both in the individual participants lives and also for the communities in which they live. As we examined in Chapter 2, the origins of Photovoice research lay firmly in this camp whereby certain marginalised groups were given the unique opportunity to tell their narratives via pictures and then to exhibit these publicly and with pride. The intention is to raise consciousness of their situation/social position and empower and even emancipate people to challenge inequality and prejudice and bring about change in communities and their own lives (Simpson and Richard 2018). Such consciousness-raising is dependent on understanding the situated, often covert, structural-institutional, relational and historical aspects of participants' lives and the dominant ways of thinking that reinforce and secure disadvantage (Baum et al. 2006).

If there is a lack of critical engagement with Photovoice, then participants who are called co-producers or co-researchers in this process of image making can potentially be politically and ethically exploited for the researchers and ultimately the policymakers'/politicians' gain. How can this be so? If researchers are the ones who ultimately write up and interpret the images and the focus-group discussions, their method is seen as empowering, but is this really so? If researchers are the ones who determine the questions to be posed during the PAR–Photovoice, they inevitably remain in power during the sessions and particularly once the sessions are over and being interpreted. The materials, themes and images are shifted, sorted, and elements extracted, but how is the participant involved and how equal is their voice if they have not been trained and enabled to play an equal part in all the stages of the project? As Sitter (2017) observes, if all of the participants are not involved in generating the research questions and later analysing and disseminating the written findings, how can they truly be seen as co-researchers? As Janes (2016) states, the power and status of academics cannot simply be redistributed, revoked, reduced or explained away in a single method, even if it takes place over a series of weeks (Simpson and Richards 2018: 4). So claims that our German project enabled real lasting change for the participants could be challenged when the perspectives of Sitter (2017) and Janes (2016) concerning true equality of status at all stages of the research, are taken into consideration. As Freire (1973/2000), discussing education, states, students/participants and teachers/researchers can only work as equals if they co-create knowledge through a process of collective introspection and dialogue. However, dialogue requires critical thinking and if this is not present, true communication cannot occur (Freire 1973/2000). This is not to say that Photovoice techniques do not enable some discussion to take place. Their value in terms of confidence building and engagement is proven from the author's multiple experiences. Yet can the researchers ever claim to grasp a complete understanding of the lives they attempt to capture?

Another well-versed criticism is that the user-friendliness of Photovoice can mislead and also be adapted and exploited as a quick and easy replacement for longer, more in-depth ethnographic engagement and immersion in fieldwork settings (Gubrium and Harper 2013: 73). The danger of delving into someone's life in this intense and emotive manner is illustrated by Freddy's experience, and maintaining a safe and nurturing environment in which to contain and support such exposure is reinforced by such incidents. The idea that anyone can run and contain a Photovoice research project is strongly disputed by the author, and, again, carefully considered and ethical approaches to this work cannot be overemphasised.

The German project was different from others in this book. All the workshops lasted one day only due to the availability of the researchers and participants. This in itself meant that when selecting the images for the exhibition, the way they were displayed, the opening lecture or talk to welcome the audience, all these stages, as with the planning stages, were done by the researchers alone. In the other projects in Ireland and England (Chapters 6 and 4) this was not the case, and in fact the researchers made the design, hanging and attendance at the exhibition part of the project. If the German project was intended to truly claim to have been PAR, then the involvement of the participants in all phases of the research would have been necessary. However, another point which mitigates this lack of involvement was that many of those in the German study were sex offenders who did not want to present themselves in the public domain and felt safer allowing the researchers to lead the public side of the research, speaking on their behalf and choosing not to attend the exhibition (all participants were invited but all declined).

The Exhibition

The exhibition in Dortmund displayed images from all the groups involved in the German project, namely: the halfway house for paroled prisoners, the legal aid centre for drugs and alcohol-related offenders and the open prisoners' group. All offenders' work was displayed, and the project was described and the findings analysed by Christine Graebsch and translated into English for the audience as well. The audience comprised social workers and students as well as interested practitioners, policymakers and academics. The debates and the reaction to the photographs received media attention and the technique was applauded widely. Yet when we critically reflect on who benefited most from the research, it was inevitably not those participants giving their time and creativity freely. To claim that their individual situations were greatly changed would be misleading, although their perspectives were made known to the limited degree we have argued applies to this project.

Conclusion

The photographs and quotations from the discussions demonstrate the effectiveness and the powerful nature of Photovoice and provide important insights on how supervision is perceived by its recipients. The professional perspective and intentions may often focus on help and support even though it's within a context of enforcement, yet for the participants of our study, these were just two themes among others. Many of the themes not explored in depth in this chapter were present in the other studies covered in this book, those of hopelessness and depression; time wasted and lost; limited freedom, control, barriers and pervasive punishment; stigmatisation, social decline and reduced citizenship and infantilisation; rubbish and debris (Fitzgibbon et al. 2017).

However, there were more hopeful aspects of regeneration, ideas of building a new life from the knowledge gained from the waste and debris and of writing a new narrative, as desistance literature reinforces and highlights (Maruna 2001). The study demonstrated participants' longing for help and their aspirations, but also the feeling that help has to be sought elsewhere, and not self-generated, and that it is precarious and can be taken away at any time. This resonates with the fundamental lack of trust generated by the process of going through the criminal justice system. It may also be possible to suggest that the, supposedly, helping hand of probation staff may be perceived by participants as infantilising and patronising guardianship and ultimately incapacitation. Finally, it was clear that the participants were sensitive about being stigmatised and held a strong sense of shame and self-loathing at times.

The study also revealed how, at least some of, the supervisees were aware of the "tick-box approach" used by the probation service. Discussions suggested that it led them to *close up* and deny the trust that is an essential precondition for supporting a process of desistance and risk analysis.

While the results of the study are necessarily preliminary, conclusions can be drawn with respect of the usefulness of a photo-based methodology. The aspects that have been raised could, of course, have emerged without the use of any photo technique as well. But the use of the Photovoice very quickly created an atmosphere that allowed the participants to go straight to the point—to the point *they* wanted to make. It gave them some time to think about the subject before the discussion in a playful as well as creative way. The photographs bridged the gap between researchers and the participants, who were regarded as co-researchers. While the use of interviews in research with people under community supervision may be too similar to an interrogation or at least a meeting with the probation officer, Photovoice techniques can make a difference. They may tease out creativity and can facilitate empowerment. However, as this chapter has cautioned, the use of Photovoice is not a quick and easy fix and needs careful consideration in terms of the ethical and social costs as well as the potential challenges such a visual technique can pose. This theme will be returned to in the next chapters that examine other studies utilising this approach.

References

Baum, F., MacDougall, C. and Smith, D. (2006) "Participatory action research," *Journal of Epidemiology & Community Health*, 60(10), pp. 854–857.

Bieker, R. (1982) "Die Adressatenperspektive: Eine empirische Untersuchung zur Genese und Implementation strafrechtlicher Sanktionsnormen am Beispiel der Bewährungshilfe und der Führungsaufsicht" [The addressees' perspective: an empirical study of the genesis and implementation of criminal sanctions exemplified by probation and supervision of conduct], *Kriminologisches Journal*, 3, pp. 205–212.

Cornel, H. (2000) "Probanden der Bewährungshilfe für Jugendliche und Heranwachsende in Berlin: Eine Untersuchung ihrer Lebenslage und ihrer Errwartungen an das Hilfesystem [Offenders under probation and adolescents in Berlin: a study of their life situation and expectations of the support system)], *Bewährungshilfe: Soziales, Strafrecht, Kriminalpolitik*, 3, pp. 302–321.

Durnescu, I. (2011) "Pains of probation: Effective practice and human rights," *International Journal of Offender Therapy and Comparative Criminology*, 55(4), pp. 530–545.

Fitzgibbon, D.W. (2008) "Fit for purpose? OASys assessments and parole decisions," *Probation Journal*, 55(1), pp. 37–51.

Fitzgibbon, W., Graebsch, C. and McNeill, F. (2017) "Pervasive punishment" in Brown, M., & Carrabine, E. (Eds.) *Routledge international handbook of visual criminology*, London: Routledge. pp. 305–319.

Freire, P. (1973) *Education for Critical Consciousness*. Vol. 1. London: Bloomsbury.

Graebsch, C. and Burkhardt, S.U. (2015) *Comparatively human? Outpatient sanctions as an alternative to deprivation of liberty from a European perspective*. Wiesbaden: VS Springer.

Graebsch, C., von Borstel, M. and Burkhardt, S.U. (2014) "Annex II: Experiencing supervision: Country Report Germany" in *Ambulant sanctions as an alternative to imprisonment in the European Union*. Sofia: Center for the Study of Democracy, pp. 95–120. Available at: http://csd.bg/artShow. php?id=1715 5.

Gubrium, A. and Harper, K. (2013) *Participatory Visual and Digital Methods*. Walnut Creek, CA.: Left Coast Press.

Janes, J.E. (2016) "Democratic encounters? Epistemic privilege, power, and community-based participatory action research," *Action Research*, 14(1), pp. 72–87.

Jehle, J.-M. (2015) *Criminal Justice in Germany: Facts and Figures*. 6th edn. Berlin: Federal Ministry of Justice and Consumer Protection.

Klug, W. and Schaitl, H. (2012) *Soziale Dienste der Justiz. Perspektiven aus Wissenschaft und Praxis*. Godesberg: Forum Verlag.

Maruna, S. (2001) *Making Good: How Ex-Convicts Reform and Rebuild Their Lives*. Washington, DC: American Psychological Association.

McNeill, F. (2013) "Community sanctions and European penology," in Daems, T., Snacken, S. and Van Zyl Smit, D. (eds.) *European penology?* Oxford; Portland, OR: Hart Publishing, pp. 170–192.

McNeill, F. and Beyens, K. (2016) *Offender Supervision in Europe*. COST Action IS1106. Glasgow: University of Glasgow, p. 11.

Morgenstern, C. (2015) "Der Resozialisierungsgrundsatz. Social reintegration as the dominant narrative for community punishment in Germany," in Robinson, G. and McNeill, F. (eds.) *Community punishment. A European perspective*. London: Routledge, pp. 72–94.

Morris, N. and Tonry, M. (1990) *Between Prison and Probation: Intermediate Punishments in a Rational Sentencing System*. Oxford: Oxford University Press.

Phelps, M.S. (2017) "Mass probation: Toward a more robust theory of state variation in punishment," *Punishment & Society*, 19(1), pp. 53–73.

Simpson, P. and Richards, M. (2018) "Using Photovoice with working-class men: Affordances, contradictions and limits to reflexivity," *Qualitative Research in Psychology*, 1, pp. 1–21.

Sitter, K.C. (2017) "Taking a closer look at Photovoice as a Participatory Action Research Method," *Journal of Progressive Human Services*, 28(1), pp. 36–48.

Tjettmers, T. and Henning, T. (2016) *Grundbildung im Strafvollzug. Bedarfe, Bedingungen und Ziele.* [Basic education in the penal system. Needs, conditions and goals]. Bielefeld: Bertelsmann Verlag.

6   Ireland and the Probation Centre

This chapter reviews a project undertaken at a probation centre in Ireland which utilised Photovoice to foreground the experiences of probationers on their journey towards desistance. The project aimed to explore the difficulties they face such as stigma, social judgement and exclusion together with their need for emotional calm, support and understanding both from their supervisors and from the wider community.

As noted in the previous chapter, the context for the project was the growth of "mass supervision" across the EU and the research initiative organised by COST. The importance of Ireland as a case study is that by comparison with some other European countries, certainly with England and Wales, Irish probation appears still embedded in welfare-oriented approaches. Deirdre Healy (2016) found that Irish probationers appreciated practical assistance with personal problems, opportunities to enhance human and social capital through participation in rehabilitation programmes, and strong professional relationships with probation officers. One participant in her study powerfully illustrated the value of relationship-based practice in his comment:

> [my probation officer is] a nice kind of guy and I wouldn't want to let him down. I'd feel bad coz he wouldn't give out really, he'd just say "Ah, what have you done?" or "This is not good," you know. But he would be strict enough as well.
>
> (Healy 2016: 61)

Though offender supervision in Ireland is still predominantly welfare centred, some signs of a punitive shift have emerged over the past decade or so. For instance, actuarial risk assessment tools were introduced in 2006 and the Probation Service explicitly subordinates rehabilitation to public protection in their " "vision" statement—"Safer communities

DOI: 10.4324/9781003017127-6

and fewer victims through offender rehabilitation" (Probation Service 2015: 5). Nevertheless, senior policymakers have publicly rejected punitive ideologies. Michael Donnellan, former director of the Probation Service and current director of the Irish Prison Service, stated in an interview with Healy:

> People who come into prison are broken people and the task is: do you break them further by humiliating them or do you say "our job now is to help fix you back up"? And I completely believe that [it's] our job to fix people back up.
>
> (Donnellan and Healy 2014: 24)

The primary legislation governing probation supervision in Ireland remained for decades the Probation of Offenders Act 1907, legislation which pre-dates Irish independence from the UK. Despite some notable developments (such as the introduction of community service orders under the Criminal Justice [Community Service] Act 1983), the history of the Irish Probation Service has been characterised overwhelmingly by continuity rather than change (Healy 2015). Despite a growing preoccupation with public protection and risk management in probation discourse, the penal welfare narrative remains dominant and probation officers' primary function is still to 'advise, assist and befriend' offenders. Managerial preoccupations are largely symbolic. For example, probation officers continue to prioritise clinical judgement over actuarial risk assessment (Bracken 2010). Nonetheless, the pace of change began to accelerate with the Criminal Justice (Community Sanctions) Bill introduced in February 2014 which will replace the 1907 Act, although it is still (2022) working its way through the legislative system. The Bill "will provide a modern statement of the law governing community sanctions and the role of the Probation Service in the criminal justice system" (Department of Justice 2020). The Bill retains penal welfare ideals (for example, probation officers must possess social work qualifications) but also includes references to risk, responsibility and public protection.

Although the penal landscape in Ireland is reasonably well researched at the macro level, studies of the supervision experience from the perspective of probationers are relatively rare. In one of few available studies, Healy (2016) discovered that the majority of probationers responded favourably to supervision, which, in their eyes, was still underpinned by welfare ideals. Probationers appreciated practical assistance with issues such as employment and addiction, as well as opportunities to enhance their skills and positive social networks through rehabilitation or educational programmes. Relationships based on respect, concern and acceptance helped probationers gain insight into their offending behaviour and deal with feelings of shame about their offences. A minority found probation unhelpful, either because external events undermined their capacity to engage or because they found supervision inconvenient, controlling or intrusive. Seymour (2013) also found that young people valued their relationships with probation officers, particularly when they received non-judgemental support and encouragement, and appreciated officers' willingness and ability to access services on their behalf. However, despite these positive assessments, probationers in both studies concluded that probation did not directly cause desistance either because a backdrop of socio-economic problems limited its impact or because change was perceived as an internal developmental process (Fitzgibbon and Healy 2019: 3).

Setting up the Project

A key aim of this project was therefore to explore the utility of Photovoice as a tool for researching the lived experience of supervision in different sociocultural and penal contexts and to make the invisible visible by creating a set of visual representations of the supervision experience. As Fitzgibbon, Graebsch and McNeill (2017) note, there are few iconic images that evoke this experience, making it difficult to imagine what it *feels* like to be under supervision. The Irish study is, like the others discussed in this book, embedded in the emerging field of visual criminology (Hayward and Presdee 2010), which sees images as offering a powerful way of "seeing" crime and crime control. Images are not simply objective representations of reality but can be interpreted in multiple, subjective and even contradictory ways, as different audiences engage with and ascribe meaning to them (see Chapter 8 for a detailed discussion of this issues). The aim of this project was that these images could provide a window onto the experience of supervision for those subject to it and also for the wider public for whom supervision is often invisible or inaccessible in terms of its purpose. The aim was to provide Irish probationers with an opportunity to share their lived experiences of supervision through photographs and discussion. While the photographs are treated as research artefacts in their own right, their meanings are also interpreted via a shared, collaborative dialogue between participants, the researcher and the audience.

The Irish study followed more or less the same procedures as the others described in this book. Eight men under probation supervision and attending a probation-funded, community-based rehabilitation programme decided to take part in the study. They were invited to participate in a day-long workshop of photography and discussion. Following a briefing session where the project was explained in detail, participants were provided with digital cameras and given guidance on how to use them. They were then given an hour to take ten pictures that captured their experience of supervision. The photos were developed into hard-copy prints and returned to the participants, who were asked to think about why they chose the image and what it represented. In focus groups they shared their thoughts and feelings around the photo(s) and were given an opportunity to identify a caption and description. Permissions were sought from the co-researchers for the publication and reproduction of photographs at sites of audiencing (see Chapter 8). The photographs were returned or kept with the participants' permission at the end of the project. Ethical approval was obtained from the universities and from agencies that facilitated the research. In total, the eight participants produced 84 images and provided captions for 31 of these (Fitzgibbon and Healy 2019).

There were of course practical ethical considerations—as distinct from the general ones discussed in Chapter 3, and although they apply to all the projects, it is worth noting them here. For example copyright issues need to be carefully considered and adequate permissions must be sought from the photographers to reproduce or exhibit the images. Photographs need to be returned or kept with permission of the co-researchers at the end of the project. These considerations were taken into account in the current project. Before the fieldwork began, the researchers clearly explained the project to participants, including the ethical protocols governing the research and the potential uses of the images. Participants then had an opportunity to discuss the project with the researchers and were asked to sign a consent form indicating their willingness to participate. Pseudonyms are used throughout this case study to protect participants' privacy.

Interpreting the Photographs

In this section, the visual analysis of the photographs produced by participants will be summarised and then the narrative analysis of their focus-group transcripts will be discussed. We shall then conclude with some general observations about conducting the research.

The key overarching themes that were identified were: (a) *Help and support*, the balance between the provision of assistance and the imposition of undue constraints; (b) *Time, nature and growth*, the distinction between quality time and wasted, or suspended, time; (c) *Stigma and judgement*, the challenges associated with social exclusion, stigmatisation and labelling; and (d) *Transitions and beginnings*, the challenges associated with shedding obsolete criminal and adolescent values and labels. These findings were originally discussed in Fitzgibbon and Healy's article "Lives and Spaces" (Fitzgibbon and Healy 2019).

Help and Support

The first theme, *help and support*, concerned participants' experiences of their supervision experiences, all of which were positive. Participants mostly focused on their experiences with the probation-funded programme they were attending at the probation centre rather than one-to-one meetings with individual probation officers. In particular, they cited opportunities to learn new skills, engage in creative self-expression and develop supportive peer and professional networks as particularly engaging and enriching. Many of their photographs depicted the abundant opportunities for personal learning and development within the programme and included images of the library, art room, educational facilities and the horticultural area. Photographs of probationers' mosaics and paintings which adorn the walls of the building were especially common. Jack, who captured this image of the art room, commented, "it's not basically about art. It's just [...] about change, like, learning and change, like to change your life." Here, the paint-splattered table is covered with well-worn artist palettes, brushes and paints, while the wall behind the table displays printed images that perhaps represent ideas for future art projects. The handbag sitting in full view on the table suggests a level of trust between staff and participants.

Daniel's explanation for his love of art was particularly poignant:

> the art room is deadly, have brilliant craic [fun] in there. It's deadly what they do. It just makes my day. Like I was depressed out of my life before I started art. And I mean depressed to bits, cut myself, the whole lot. [...] Now it wouldn't be something that come into my head.

Conor also emphasised the transformative power of art: "there's other things that people have done, put other work on canvases. Like this one here [...] could be an inspiration for someone to work on something like that." Creative work thus appeared to serve several purposes: facilitating personal development and change, calming difficult emotions and inspiring change in others. The men's experiences in this regard call to mind the principles of strengths-based rehabilitation

Figure 6.1 It's Never Too Late to Learn by Jack

models which are designed to enhance creative potential and develop probationers' talents, skills and resources (see e.g. Woldgabreal et al. 2014).

Professional relationships with programme staff were also highly valued by the men. Jack was able to explain this: "people are listening to you, to your problems, and help you with your day-to-day [...] Without them I don't think I'd be here." The attitudes of probation workers marked a welcome departure from the stigmatising and detached relationships probationers had experienced in prison. As Conor noted,

> [to prison officers] you're only a number. They throw things back in your face then. When things happen to them then they'd be wondering "oh why did that happen? Why did he attack them?" [...] They want to treat you like a dog, you're going to act like a dog.

Additionally, the men valued the informal emotional support offered by peers within the programme, a bond that is largely unacknowledged in studies of probation supervision. The canteen served as a forum for informal discussions between probationers, which strengthened their social bonds and aided the therapeutic process. It is therefore unsurprising that this room appeared in a number of photographs. Jack observed: "spending time with people like that, not crime or [...] just for the sake of all being here on the same page trying to help each other. And not having to gain something from interacting, not gaining something, money or whatever." Though criminological researchers have traditionally focused on the negative impact of peer associations, the significance of prosocial peer support is widely recognised in the desistance literature for generating a range of benefits, including the opportunity to learn from the experience of similarly situated others and to encounter living exemplars of successful change (Weaver 2013). The other aspect of the probation centre that received praise and recognition was that staff and probationers shared meals together in this canteen space, another aspect that humanised and supported positive interaction and self-esteem.

Overall, the images and commentary suggest that the probation programme was viewed favourably and perceived to be encouraging the development of active, collaborative and humane relationships between service providers, in this case the staff at the probation centre and the service users, those on supervision (McCulloch et al. 2016). Such

Figure 6.2 Canteen by Conor

nurturing and positive relationships are thought to enhance the effectiveness of supervision (Kennealy et al. 2012). High satisfaction rates with probation supervision are not unusual in the Irish context, perhaps as a result of the long-standing commitment to welfarism (see Healy 2015 for further details).

Time, Nature and Growth

Time emerged as a central theme, particularly among the older men who distinguished between "quality" and "wasted" time. This theme resonates with the other studies in Chapters 4 and 5. While a prison term was widely regarded as "lost" time, time spent out of prison and under supervision was almost universally experienced as meaningful time. Jack, who had only recently been released from prison, took the following image of a family in the park to represent this experience.

Periods of imprisonment were largely experienced as lost or wasted time, and there was a perception that time accelerated in prison as participants missed out on important family events and developmental milestones. Conversely, time spent under supervision was almost universally experienced as quality time, not only because people were

Figure 6.3 Never Take the Little Things for Granted by Jack

Figure 6.4 Untitled by Daniel

able to engage in meaningful activities but also because they were free to spend time with their families and rebuild trusting and important relationships which had often suffered due to absence or loss of trust through offending. Having the time to reflect and cultivate feelings of peace and stillness, often through engagement with the natural world, was particularly important to participants. Daniel commented in relation to an image of a planter (see Figure 6.4),

> that was like life and freedom, to be able to pick up a flower and f***in' smell it. To be able to plant a flower, look at the colours of them. Just to be able to sit there and look at them. I love stuff like that.

In conversation, Daniel contrasted the quality of time spent with family with his experience of prison, explaining, "When I'm on my own or even with the wife and kids in the park, you don't have time like that [in prison]. Quality time." He elaborated,

> Freedom yeah, time to think. Things you missed, just simple things like a park, time to yourself. [In prison] you're not even thinking,

you're that wasted. You're not even seeing what you're missing like. Life is just going by you like, life is just whizzing by.

Although the men attempted to keep busy to pass the time in prison, this was not directed towards achievement of substantial goals. Community sentences, on the other hand, which encouraged them to engage in meaningful activities and allowed them to spend quality time with their families, created a more lasting impression. As Daniel observed, "you do it in here [prison] to keep yourself occupied, you do it out here [probation] to get what you want." Their impermanent experiences are consistent with O'Donnell's (2014) research, which found that prisoners often experience prison time as sluggish, meaningless and boring, seeming to move slowly as it is lived but accelerating in retrospect due to the absence of memorable or meaningful events.

The emphasis on quality time was closely intertwined with time spent in natural environments which elicited feelings of tranquillity, peace and well-being. The men's photographs frequently included images of the natural world such as flowers, parks, lakes, rivers, fish and ducks.

Conor described being put at ease on his first day at the programme by spending a few moments in stillness, watching the fish. He continued, "it is a nervous experience. You're coming into a place you mightn't know anyone. So you sit there and relax for a couple of minutes. [...] You can sit there, sit in the chairs and look at the fish." He later commented on the value of having time and space to reflect: "if you haven't got relaxation or any time to think, you're always on the go, your mind is doing a hundred things that it shouldn't be doing." Daniel also appreciated the healing power of natural environments:

> Well I would have took pictures of the park definitely because see that family playing, time to be by yourself, on your own. And the mountains, definitely a picture of the mountains would have gone in coz that's where I go when my head is melted.

It is likely that experiences of the drab and artificial prison environment enhance and accentuate the vibrancy, beauty and colour of the natural world. As Jack commented, "[you] can't see trees [in prison], green, there's nothing just high walls on either side of you." The men's efforts to find a space for peace and quietude in their lives support the growing criminological literature on the intersection between boredom and criminality (Torbenfeldt Bengtsson 2012). Doing nothing can generate frustration but, in different circumstances, can also foster reflection, a sense of well-being and creativity (Kets de Vries 2014). Moreover, meaningful contact with the natural world is increasingly recognised as an effective therapeutic tool (e.g. Jordan 2014).

Stigma and Judgement

The third theme, *stigma and judgement*, highlighted the structural challenges faced by probationers on the journey towards desistance. These included social exclusion, stigma and labelling. Participants' lives were negotiated within an environment underpinned by criminality, and so they felt personally tainted by the negative attitudes and damaged reputation of their community. Their photographs also reflected the temptations, as well as the dangers, that surrounded them including addiction, petty offending and homelessness. Adam, who photographed an alleyway frequented by a local homeless man (Figure 6.5), observed, "I think that's really sad, with your man drying out his sleeping bag." Michael responded, "that's across the road from the lovely little park as well. And he's like hidden in the corner." The hidden underbelly of the dispossessed and marginalised was captured in many of the images.

Figure 6.5 Untitled by Michael

One of the prominent themes that emerged from the photographs concerned the issue of place. Hunter and Farrall (2015) observed that the subjective meanings assigned to particular places can provide important insights into people's lives and sense of self. It is telling therefore that the men viewed their surroundings in primarily negative terms and appeared to feel tainted, at least to some extent, by association. In conversation, they saw their community as having two faces, the clean, prosperous and attractive public facade concealing a darker reality. This spatial dissonance was also reflected in their photographs, which included images of rubbish, graffiti, homelessness and crime juxtaposed with images of well-maintained local parks and public artworks (Fitzgibbon and Healy 2019: 10). One example (Figure 6.6) was this photograph of the local park with statutes on display taken by Luke.

Adam, who chose to photograph the same shot as Luke, expanded upon their intended meanings: "kids singing and dancing, that's not happening [...] So it's the contrast of it. It's just the dirt, it's just hid away. This is on display, all the happy stuff is on display." Michael agreed, saying, "In behind the door then, you have this. It's a shock. It's a skip like." Criminality also formed a backdrop to everyday life for these men. Luke, who photographed the front page of a newspaper

Figure 6.6 Untitled by Luke

Figure 6.7   Untitled by Adam

containing a report of a gangland murder, observed "that's what's going on every day in day to day life. [...] Don't feel anything [about it], to be honest. It's bad but it's what happens."

The important of place and the community could be explained at least partly by the micro-politics of life in socially disadvantaged urban neighbourhoods. Despite a history of disadvantage, the majority of social housing neighbourhoods in Ireland subsequently evolved into 'liveable' environments due to government-sponsored regeneration schemes and a favourable macro-economic environment (Norris 2014). However, the transition is not complete and therefore there remain pockets of deprivation. It was significant how the members of both groups stressed their compassion for vulnerable people, perhaps to distance themselves from their community's negative reputation or perhaps due to the closeness of their precarious situation to these "others." During the fieldwork, members of the first group helped an alcoholic woman get home safely, while a member of the second group expressed sympathy towards a homeless man he encountered while taking his photographs. This interpretation is consistent with existing research which shows that residents in stigmatised communities often stress their prosocial values and behaviours in order to separate themselves from stigmatising labels (Ilan 2011; see also Wacquant 2015).

As in Hunter and Farrall's (2015) sample, the men in this project appear to have altered their meanings and emotional attachments linked to their surroundings in order to facilitate their progress towards desistance. The probation programme was viewed as a safe haven away from this tainted environment, which provided a nurturing environment within which to create and act out a new identity.

Transitions and Beginnings

This leads to the final theme to be covered within this chapter, that of *transitions and beginnings*. The participants focused within some of their images on the transitions to a crime-free identity and to adulthood more generally. The images created within the project often referenced ideas relating to new beginnings and personal transformation. However, this was rarely straightforward and many of the photographs captured their experiences of the criminal justice system, suggesting their criminal pasts were still present or still suspended over them to some extent. Jack's images of the criminal justice system juxtaposed with images of families playing in a local park, highlighted this sense of transition and search for a new beginning. He remarked "the gardaí [Irish police] I don't want to see. That's me past, I want to leave that behind. There's where I want to go, my family" (see Figure 6.3 above). The older men, often after serving long stretches in prison, like Jack, focused on adult masculine pursuits (e.g. family life, non-materialistic values).

Interestingly, the younger men's photographs reflected adolescent masculine values and pursuits (e.g. gambling, nice cars, money and alcohol). The images produced by the younger cohort in the project included pictures of "nice" cars, handfuls of cash, pub interiors, the local betting shop and alcohol displays in shop windows. Two co-researchers even described stopping to place bets during their fieldwork when taking their photographs. These preoccupations are reminiscent of street culture, which promotes an identity centred on consumerism, hedonism, spontaneity and freedom (Wright and Decker 2011).

Images of alcohol were particularly common. Michael took a photograph of a shop window display of beer cans as well as an image of spirits, and acknowledged the links between alcohol and crime when he stated, "don't get me wrong, I'd prefer to drink spirits like but [...] charges seem to come a lot faster with it." In the discussion about Sean's photograph, which showed him adopting a triumphant pose in front of the same shop window display, Luke noted, "he [Sean] likes Carlsberg, or Budweiser, yeah" with Sean concurring, "yeah, I enjoy the beer." That the men choose to photograph large quantities of alcohol on display rather than single bottles or cans suggests an attraction to excess, consumerism and hedonism, values usually associated with criminality. However, the young people in this sample appeared to have stopped offending. It may be that their ongoing identification with street culture provided a sense of self-continuity as they made the transition from criminality to desistance. This possibility is supported by the ambiguities evident in some of their images—for example, Adam's photograph of the sun breaking through dark clouds and Luke's of a painting portraying a turbulent sky overshadowing a colourful cityscape.

The older co-researchers were dismissive of such values, with Jack for example criticising young prisoners for always being "on the phone 'Get me runners, get me tracksuits.'" Instead their images were suggestive of identity transitions and new beginnings. Conor photographed a blank canvas:

> because everything is blank. You have to paint your own picture. […] You'll have so much of it painted onto a canvas, you'll have to finish it and it's all about yourself. But for me, Jack and I, coming out of a prison we're starting off with a blank canvas. If we want people to trust us, we want our family to trust us and earn their trust and we have their trust now because we're coming here.

Yet images associated with the criminal justice system such as police cars, solicitors' offices, the courthouse and, of course, the probation office, were also common across both groups. For the older men in particular, these acted as a reminder of a criminal past that they were attempting to leave behind. Daniel's rejection of the criminal mentality is evident in his comment that "another thing about having a conversation within someone in prison and like, youze are all obviously in prison. It always ends up back talking about like […] war stories. […] We never talk about war stories or anything like that [in the programme]." The criminal justice imagery also seemed to prompt reflections on a feared future self. Jack's anxieties are evident in his comments about prisoners serving life sentences:

> you'd never be right coming out. I don't think you'd ever be able to re-adjust back into normal life after being locked up all them years. You'd be like a robot. It would be so frightening I'd say coming back out.

Together, desired and feared future selves assist desistance by fostering the hope of a better future, acting as a reminder that change is possible and providing a blueprint for action (see also Healy 2016, Maruna 2001). The closeness of the desired goals versus the feared future serves to highlight the challenges facing these co-researchers in their stated aim to leave criminality behind and desist in the future.

Reflecting on the Photographs

Though the visual and narrative themes were identified by the researchers, the meanings attributed to the images by the co-researchers were foregrounded in the coding process where possible (i.e. where the images were discussed during the focus-group sessions). The analytic approach thus generated multiple levels of meaning and captured the perspectives of the researchers, the researched and other audiences. This process results in the images no longer being the primary source of meaning since they become theorised as icons through which a range of meanings are created as viewers bring their own social and cultural understandings to the images (Rose 2011). The ability to produce multilayered understandings of a phenomenon is a key strength of the Photovoice technique.

It was clear from the focus-group discussions that the method quickly engaged participants, who showed increased confidence in their ability to select images and engage in self-advocacy. By enabling probationers to tap into their creativity and gain photography skills, the projects facilitated the sharing of power. This differs fundamentally from traditional research where power often lies solely with the researcher and also from probationers' experiences of supervision where the rules are laid down by the supervisor.

Visual imagery encourages people to question taken-for-granted ideas, explore emotions and highlight issues that might not otherwise have come to light. In our experience, asking people to explore their reasons for taking particular photographs prompted them to reflect more deeply on their personal experiences, something that was recognised by Jack, who observed:

> Weird, to be honest, I didn't think the pictures would have brought that much out of me. Made me think that much. [...] For the first twenty minutes I was walking around with the camera, thinking "what am I going to take a picture of?" It's hard to get your head around it what you're going to take a picture of. To be honest, I was clueless thinking "what is this about?" When you take it and you

see the picture and you start talking about them, it's surprising how much you get from the picture.

Interestingly, the approach also proved effective in terms of engaging participants who were reluctant to discuss emotions during the focus-group sessions. Two of the younger men in particular were quite reticent, but still captured evocative images that effectively communicated their feelings, preoccupations and experiences (see Figures 6.3 and 6.7 which were taken by one of the younger men).

In addition, we found that the method shed new light on previously undocumented aspects of supervision by enabling participants to reflect on abstract, implicit or complex concepts that would not normally feature on standard interview schedules.

Ultimately, the research told us as much about participants' lives in general as it did about their supervision experiences in particular. While some might consider this a limitation of the study, we discovered that enabling participants to become the experts and leaders in this process provided rich insights into their lifeworlds and raised interesting questions about where to draw the boundary between supervision and its wider social, organisational and personal contexts. Traditionally, researchers attempted to study the supervision experience in isolation. That is, they are studied only in relation to regular meetings with a probation officer. However, people subject to supervision do not necessarily experience the sanction in this way, as the supervision experience is inextricably shaped by what is happening in people's lives outside the probation office (see also Shapland et al. 2012). For example, past experiences with the criminal justice system could colour perceptions of a current supervision order.

Different Ways of Seeing

The final advantage of techniques such as Photovoice discussed here is its capacity to accommodate multiple voices and perspectives, including those of the photographers who capture the image, the researchers who try to discern patterns in the images and offer theoretical interpretations, and the audiences who interact with the images in exhibition spaces. Photovoice can be transformative and we found that audiences engaged enthusiastically with the images during the exhibitions. Chapter 8 looks at this in detail and as a new method of generating data, audiencing. While the overall themes that emerged from the audience reactions were very consistent with the meanings attributed to the images by the photographers, differences emerged in relation to specific photographs.

The photograph of the goldfish bowl shown earlier provides a good illustration of the variety of meanings that can be assigned to a single image by different observers.

The Exhibition

A photographic exhibition of the images was held at the probation centre. The exhibition was attended by a range of academics, practitioners and policymakers and some of the photographers. Audience members at the exhibitions were given a printout of the images and asked to record their interpretations of the photographs (this is discussed in detail in Chapter 8).

Despite the use of digital cameras—it was discovered that disposable cameras with film had too long a turnaround time in terms of film development and printing—some of the photographs produced by participants were blurred or unfocused, raising questions about their usability. However, it was decided that all photographs, including so-called mistakes, were valuable contributions and so they were exhibited. These photographs were accepted and there were no negative comments about them. This indicated that the audience agreed that the message being communicated by the images is more important than the quality of the photograph.

Another equally important issue concerned anonymity. The issue has been raised in a previous chapter. Though participants were advised not to take photographs that could potentially identify people, some captured photographs that identified themselves, or the research setting. For instance, several took photographs of a well-known bronze statue in a local park (Figure 6.6). Scholars sometimes avoid publishing such images, which arguably takes control away from participants and prevents important messages from entering the public domain. Alternatively, identifying features can be removed or altered using photo editing software, but the results can sometimes be dehumanising. Ultimately, we decided to exclude images that identified people but tried to incorporate their messages in other ways (e.g. through publishing participants' contributions to the focus-group discussions) so that we, and others, could learn from their experiences.

Conclusion

The Irish study deployed an innovative research method—Photovoice—to gain novel insights into the lived experience of people under probation supervision. The analysis identified several important themes, including the significance of practical and emotional support, the need for time to be meaningfully spent, and the desire for peace and emotional calm. The findings also shed light on the challenges faced by those on probation supervision while they struggle to regain a purchase in the community and take steps towards desistance. These included exposure to stigma, exclusion and social judgement, as well as the difficulties associated with transitioning to a crime-free identity.

The method also provided important insights into participants' perceptions of the positive features of the supervision experience. The Irish co-researchers valued the welfarist, or rehabilitative, features of supervision such as emotional and practical support, collaborative relationships and meaningful rehabilitation activities. Their experiences resonate with existing Irish interview-based research, such as Healy's (2012) study, which found that the majority of probationers viewed supervision favourably. They particularly valued practical assistance with issues such as unemployment, strong professional relationships with their supervisors and opportunities to engage in meaningful activities. Photovoice is, of course, quite capable of identifying the more "painful" dimensions of supervision (see Fitzgibbon et al. 2017).

Furthermore, the Photovoice technique generated insights that went beyond the findings produced by more traditional methods, suggesting that it can offer new ways to study the lived experience of supervision. The Irish study revealed unexpected findings such as the importance of wider contextual issues such as place, identity and culture in Ireland. While some might regard the resultant emphasis on probationers' lives in general rather than their experience of supervision in particular as a weakness of the method, it could also be argued that the findings highlight the need to study the impact of wider social forces on individual supervision experiences. Indeed, it is widely recognised that probation supervision does not occur in a vacuum and individuals' actions are inevitably shaped by the social structures that encompass them (Farrall et al. 2011). Photovoice may thus constitute an effective way to explore the supervision experience *within* its social, political and cultural contexts.

References

Bracken, D. (2010) "Skills and knowledge for contemporary probation practice," *Irish Probation Journal*, 50(1), pp. 101–114.

Criminal Justice (Community Service) Act (1983) Available at: www.irishstatutebook.ie/eli/1983/act/23/enacted/en/print

Department of Justice (2020) *Criminal Justice (Community Sanctions) Bill*. Dublin: Department of Justice. Available at: www.justice.ie/en/JELR/Pages/Criminal_Justice_(Community_Sanctions)_Bill

Donnellan, M. and Healy, D. (2014) "Michael Donnellan, Director General, Irish Prison Service, Republic of Ireland (interview by Deirdre Healy)," in Hurley, M.H. and Das D.K. (eds.) *Trends in corrections: Interviews with corrections leaders around the world*. Vol. 2. London: Routledge, pp. 17–34.

Farrall, S., Sharpe, G., Hunter, B. and Calverley, A. (2011) "Theorizing structural and individual-level processes in desistance and persistence: Outlining an integrated perspective," *Australian and New Zealand Journal of Criminology*, 44(2), pp. 218–234.

Fitzgibbon, W. and Healy, D. (2019) "Lives and spaces: Photovoice and offender supervision in Ireland and England," *Criminology & Criminal Justice*, 19(1), pp. 3–25.

Fitzgibbon, W., Graebsch, C. and McNeill, F. (2017) "Pervasive punishment: Experiencing supervision" in Carrabine, E. (ed.) *Routledge handbook of visual criminology*. Abingdon: Routledge, pp. 305–319.

Hayward, K. and Presdee, M. (2010) (eds.) *Framing Crime: Cultural Criminology and the Image*. Abingdon: Routledge.

Healy, D. (2012) *The Dynamics of Desistance: Charting Pathways through Change*. Abingdon: Routledge.

Healy, D. (2015) "The evolution of community sanctions in the Republic of Ireland: Continuity, challenge and change," in Robinson, G. and McNeill, F. (eds.) *Community punishment in Europe*. Abingdon: Routledge, pp. 136–155.

Healy, D. (2016) "'I've always tried but I hadn't got the willpower:' Understanding pathways to desistance in the Republic of Ireland," in Shapland, J., Farrall, S. and Bottoms, A. (eds.) *Global perspectives on desistance: Reviewing what we know and looking to the future*. Abingdon: Routledge, pp. 50–65.

Hunter, B. and Farrall, S. (2015) "Space, place and desistance from drug use," *Oñati Socio-legal Series* [online], 5(3), pp. 945–968.

Ilan, J. (2011) "Reclaiming respectability? The class-cultural dynamics of crime, community and governance in inner-city Dublin," *Urban Studies*, 48(6), pp. 1137–1155.

Jordan, M. (2014) *Nature and Therapy: Understanding Counselling and Psychotherapy in Outdoor Spaces*. Abingdon: Routledge.

Kennealy, P., Skeem, J., Manchak, S. and Louden, J. (2012) "Firm, fair, and caring officer-offender relationships protect against supervision failure," *Law and Human Behavior*, 36(6), pp. 496–505.

Kets de Vries, M. (2014) "Doing nothing and nothing to do: The hidden value of empty time and boredom," *Organizational Dynamics*, 44(3), pp. 169–175.

Maruna, S. (2001) *Making Good: How Ex-convicts Reform and Rebuild Their Lives*. Washington, DC: American Psychological Association.

McCulloch, T., with members of Positive Prison? Positive Futures (2016) "Co-producing justice sanctions? Citizen perspectives," *Criminology and Criminal Justice*, 16(4), pp. 431–451.

Norris, M. (2014) *Social Housing, Disadvantage and Neighbourhood Liveability: Ten Years of Change in Social Housing Neighbourhoods.* Abingdon: Routledge.

O'Donnell, I. (2014) *Prisoners, Solitude and Time.* Oxford: OUP.

Probation Service (2015) *Strategic Plan 2015–2017.* Dublin: Stationery Office.

Rose, G. (2011) *Visual Methodologies: An Introduction to Researching with Visual Materials.* London: SAGE.

Seymour, M. (2013) *Youth Justice in Context: Community, Compliance and Young People.* Abingdon: Routledge.

Shapland, J., Bottoms, A. and Muir, G. (2012) "Perceptions of the criminal justice system among young adult would-be desisters," in Losel, F., Bottoms, A., and Farrington, D. (eds.) *Young adult offenders: Lost in transition?* Abingdon: Routledge.

Torbenfeldt Bengtsson, T. (2012) "Boredom and action—experiences from youth confinement," *Journal of Contemporary Ethnography*, 41(5), pp. 526–553.

Wacquant, L. (2015) "Revisiting territories of relegation: Class, ethnicity and state in the making of advanced marginality," *Urban Studies*, 53(6), pp. 1077–1088.

Weaver, B. (2013) "Co-producing desistance: Who works to support desistance?" in Durnescu, I. and McNeill, F. (eds.) *Understanding penal practices.* Abingdon: Routledge, pp. 193–205.

Woldgabreal, Y., Day, A. and Ward, T. (2014) "The community-based supervision of offenders from a positive psychology perspective," *Aggression and Violent Behavior*, 19(1), pp. 32–41.

Wright, R. and Decker, S. (2011) *Armed Robbers in Action: Stick Ups and Street Culture.* Boston: Northeastern University Press.

7 Working with Practitioners and Students

We said in Chapter 2 that Photovoice—and its close cousin photo-elicitation—were used in a diversity of scenarios. The method started off in public health (Wang and Burris 1997) from where it spread, as we have seen, in two directions: community mobilisation on the one hand and self-reflection on the other. Of course the "spread" analogy is only partly correct in the sense that the emergence of Photovoice-like strategies in these latter areas did not have to wait on its development in the public health area. In the chapters above we have concentrated on examples of the "self-reflection" variety of Photovoice with examples drawn mainly from probation.

But, of course, it is obvious that whether used in the context of self-reflection or community mobilisation—or indeed, combinations of the two—Photovoice is a process of learning, research and discovery: clarifying how you feel about your personal situation as a probation client or learning about how your community is oppressed. It is therefore obvious that Photovoice offers much as a general strategy in the education context, as a general learning resource for students in many areas: a teaching device which encourages critical thinking by students, in particular those learning to be practitioners. We have already seen how Photovoice projects involve organisers and participants in new and egalitarian relationships as "co-researchers." This obviously can have a profound influence both on the relations between teachers and students and on the relation between learning theory and developing practitioner skills.

This use of Photovoice in the educational context requires caution. There might arguably be a core tension built into the relationship between teachers and students verse co-researchers or "co-learners." It might be argued that the relationship between teachers and students can only go so far down this road, At the end of the day, teachers are

DOI: 10.4324/9781003017127-7

responsible for imparting a body of theory and knowledge to students. This is not in the last analysis an egalitarian relationship.

Traditional Teaching Methods

So a rather stereotyped view of traditional methods of education and training of practitioners—in probation or social work for example—might make two assumptions. Firstly, that there is a distinct body of theory which is in the possession of the teacher and which the student practitioner needs to learn. Secondly, that the theory is prior to the practice in the sense that the student needs to learn the theory and then go out and apply it in a practical setting, and in the process may come to refine and deepen their knowledge of the theory.

In probation education, student practitioners might learn—to take a not exactly uncontroversial example—that the aim of probation supervision is to minimise the risk that their clients might present to the public and to themselves. In other words, the students must assimilate the "risk paradigm." Photovoice might be incorporated into their training. They might, for example, be asked to go out and take photographs on the themes of risk and self-harm. The latter might be part of their practice education in which they go on placement in a probation office and learn the practical skills of actually applying these methods to particular individual probation clients.

In their Photovoice discussions, they might explore the various aspects of risk and self-harm. They *might* start to conclude that the most important issue is not how much risk their clients presented but how to help them back into stable lives free of crime. That is, they may move, under their own steam as it were, away from the risk paradigm and towards the rehabilitation paradigm. But they would not *necessarily* critique the risk paradigm unless it was already problematised by the theory they learned prior to their Photovoice project. And this would be up to the teachers.

In Chapter 3, we distinguished Photovoice, photo-elicitation and photo-documentation, with Photovoice as the most and photo-documentation as the least democratic in terms of the freedom of the participants to determine their own photographs and their own interpretation. We said that in photo-elicitation, and even more in photo-documentation, the organisers had the last word on the interpretation of the photographs, and that is what is happening here. The students are free to take their own photographs but the theoretical paradigm in terms of which they are to be interpreted is sacrosanct and remains in the last analysis the property of the teachers. Photovoice, used in the specific context of teaching, moves, in terms of our discussion in Chapter 2, towards the more top-down methods photo-elicitation and documentation. Many probation teachers will see this as entirely correct.

Leaving aside the whole issue of what is the correct body of theory that probation students should be learning, and leaving aside also the progressive deskilling of probation practice (see Fitzgibbon 2007), we shall now turn to look at the general debate about teaching methods and emergence of theories of pedagogy which reject the teacher as simply the passer of knowledge to the student and, instead, stress the importance of "co-learning" strategies. These latter, we shall argue, closely parallel the emergence of Photovoice as a form of democratic action-research in which the organisers and participants become, as already noted, in effect co-researchers. We shall then illustrate, through some case studies in which the author participated, how Photovoice methods might contribute to co-learning strategies, in particular in the training of probation practitioners and the extent to which the problems of the "ultimate authority" of the teacher and the dominant paradigm can be resolved without compromising Photovoice.

The Visual Image and Co-learning

There has in recent years been a blossoming of "co-learning" strategies in discussions of educational pedagogy (for the UK, see e.g. Bovill 2020). Much of the impulse for this derives from the work of the great Brazilian educator and philosopher Paulo Freire. Freire had much to say on the relations between teachers and students as co-learners. He was also very much in favour of the use of visual images as part of this egalitarian process.

Freire rejected the notion of teaching as "a process of transference of knowledge from the one teaching to the learner. This is the mechanical transference which results in machine-like memorization" (Freire 2005: 22). By contrast,

> Only insofar as learners become thinking subjects, and recognize that they are as much thinking subjects as are the teachers, is it possible for the learners to become productive subjects of the meaning or knowledge of the object. It is in this dialectic movement that teaching and learning become knowing and reknowing. The learners gradually know what they did not yet know, and the educators reknow what they knew before.
>
> (Freire 2005: 90)

Commentators on Freire have emphasised this view of the inter-action of teachers and students as a dialectical process in which both bring resources to the situation and interact. Thus, in adult literacy teaching projects, Freire

> did not ask himself: how could one teach these adults literacy? The question was rather, how to help them, using their experience and knowledge to lead them from their spontaneous, relatively unorgan-ised, pre-critical knowledge, to a more organised and critical one [...] The dichotomy of educator-educatee, teacher-student, is over-come by the dialectical unity of the two subjects, who together dis-cover the world, and together create knowledge in a dialogue.
>
> (Andreola 2006: 222–224)

A key part of this dialectical interaction between teacher and student in which both help reorganise and elaborate the thought of the other was the use of visual images. Freire deployed images in his work on teaching adult literacy in poor communities in Brazil during the 1960s. He tried to deploy visual images which related to the problems and contradictions in the situation in which learners found themselves. He called these "generative images," and he envisaged groups of teachers and learners—again in the adult literacy setting—functioning as "culture circles" involved in the collective decoding of these images (see Freire 1996: ch. 3). Freire's visual methodology as described by Landkammer (2019: 4) sounds very close to the description of a Photovoice project:

> It begins with an investigation carried out in collaboration with people from the area where the educational activity is to take place. The collaborative investigation is dedicated to identifying "gen-erative themes" that characterize the social reality of the group. Through several stages of analysis and discussion with the local co-investigators these images are "codified" into representations—visual, auditive, or mixed media (although in the projects described by Freire he used images principally). These codifications of social reality are discussed in the culture circle—the format Freire devised for learning in groups—and "decoded" by the group. By naming and describing elements within the image, and working with the words split up into syllables for literacy training, participants also analyse their socio-political situation and the structures of oppression that they are living.
>
> (Landkammer 2019: 4)

The connections with Photovoice are obvious. As Linda Liebenberg (2018) observed, Freire saw photographs as

> a mirror to communities, reflecting everyday social and political realities that impact and shape people's lives. He argued that in discussing the content of images, people are able to step back from their lives and engage more readily with the abstract. Simultaneously, however, he saw language as living and as action. Specifically, meaning is established via a process of naming through dialogue.
>
> (Liebenberg 2018: 3)

Irrespective of whether Freire is acknowledged as the originator, these techniques have been deployed widely in educational contexts as "co-learning" strategies. For example, the use of Photovoice in teaching methodology courses for sociology students was studied by researchers at the University of Saskatchewan (Schell et al. 2009). A student described the experience:

> The act of taking photographs required creativity that does not often get a chance to surface in the classroom setting. Taking pictures with the purpose of conveying meaning allowed me to discover a new way of looking at the world, and there was much careful consideration needed at this stage of the assignment as I decided what I would photograph to represent ideas. When the photographs had been taken, I then had to consider how to present my ideas, which images to use, and how to convey the meaning I attached to each.
>
> (Schell et al. 2009: 344)

Another project (Mulder and Dull 2014) looked at the role of Photovoice in postgraduate social work education in Michigan in the US. Photovoice was able to play a role in helping students develop skills in self-reflection and the handling of emotional reactions to situations encountered in social work, which are of necessity interactive between social worker and client. Students used journaling, Photovoice and group discussion with peers to reflect on their own self-development in areas which arise out of social worker and client interaction such as values, cultural competence, advocacy on behalf of clients, engagement skills with clients, ethics and personal integrity.

One important consequence of the use of Photovoice in the classroom—though it would be true for any form of Photovoice—is that students are more able to speak about their own experiences without directly implicating the legitimacy of their personal accounts. If, for example, a student talks about racism and discrimination in terms of their own direct experience, then they directly "implicate" themselves in that account and may have to relive experiences, especially if their account is challenged in discussion. But a discussion of the same themes using more non-personal forms of communication such as provided by photographs of signs or words can give the student some psychological buffering as the self is not quite a part of the picture (Chio and Fandt 2007: 488).

Teachers and Students

The key character of Photovoice, distinguishing it from other methods involving use of photographs, is the role of organiser/teacher and participant/student as "co-researchers" or "co-learners." The literature on co-learning involving Photovoice tends to stress the democratic classroom as "a more participative learning environment, and a more reflective and self-aware learning opportunity" (Chio and Fandt 2007: 487). The stress is on the changing relationship between teacher and student. Thus, the Photovoice method enabled "collaborative relationships with students more akin to a research team rather than the student-teacher relationship" (Schell et al. 2009: 341) with the aim of encouraging "greater participatory engagement between students and subject matter, knowledge, and learning" (Chio and Fandt 2007: 484).

This blurring of the roles of teacher and student—as in Photovoice generally—means that the students become much more the owners of their own knowledge and experience. This has an effect on the student's attitude towards learning and leads to increasing motivation and self-responsibility (Chio and Fandt 2007: 487). The student's right to speak is enhanced and, as noted above, the reference to photographs rather than direct experience creates a safe and interpersonal forum for students to share their thoughts. The photograph as a medium protects students from being directly exposed. The activities of taking, selecting, discussing and sharing are an indirect form of self-revelation.

Nevertheless, there are two issues that prevent the role of teacher and student becoming *identical*, the teacher as simply another co-learner or, as in other varieties of Photovoice, simply another co-researcher. Firstly, it is the responsibility of the teacher to guarantee the democratic nature of the learning process for the students. The teacher must be the guarantor of the student's right to speak and encourage weaker students to overcome their reticence, prevent stronger students from dominating the discussion and attempt to maintain that the discussion takes a logical form—that issues or themes raised are not subsequently lost or dissipated.

It is the task of the teacher to create an open and comfortable environment and forum for students to discuss and express themselves through photography. The teacher indeed learns continuously through the interaction with students how to deepen and refine their battery of techniques for generating practical learning opportunities (see Chio and Fandt 2007: 485).

However, this is a normal minimum for any form of teacher–student relationship. What is more important for the concept of co-learning is the impact on the leadership role of the teacher. In any conceivable educational project, it is the responsibility of the teacher to provide the "big picture," that is, to show where the particular student experiences may be leading and assist their location within a larger context which itself is defined by theory.

It is useful to return to Freire on this issue, as Landkammer noted, there were some criticisms of Freire precisely along the lines of the extent to which the teacher exercised a guiding hand behind the scenes:

> But there is always a danger, and some maintain that Freire was not immune to it, of How much does the "critical consciousness" that the educator wants the participants to achieve consist of ideas the educator already knows beforehand and only wants the participants to take on? What does the selection of images, their style and pictorial language say about the educator and her/his assumptions about the participants?
>
> (Landkammer 2019: 4–5)

This is, of course, getting to the heart of the contrast between photo-documentation and Photovoice in terms of who has control of the production of the image. In Photovoice it is the student/participant. Power can be exerted by the teacher/organiser at the level of discussion of the photographs. In photo-documentation and even photo-elicitation this power is all the greater since it may extend backwards into the selection of the image itself. This was the point being made about Freire. And his somewhat double-edged characterisation of this interaction as one in which the teachers come to "reknow what they knew before," while the students learn "what they did not yet know" may perhaps collide with the inherent democracy of Photovoice, particularly in the education context where there is an existing body of theory to which the students need to be assimilated.

The use of Photovoice or any other pedagogic technique in the educational context has to be seen therefore as an aid to students in reaching and understanding a body of theory that already exists and the assimilation of this knowledge, which is defined as the goal of the particular course of education undertaken. Student discussions, however imaginatively generated by the use of photography, may end up as partial and one-sided, and it is a role of the teacher to locate these discussions in the overall coherence of the "big picture." In other words, the teacher has not just to gather up and synthesise the particular experiences of the students. They have to bring out their essential dynamic and show in which direction they are leading.

In community mobilisation projects, the participants already have a sense of being oppressed, and Photovoice helps them articulate and make clear the dimensions of their oppression. This is the stage at which the organisers may provide theories of power and exploitation which may then begin to start to make sense to the participants. However, this may not necessarily occur. The organisers might prioritise ethnic and gender oppression and the participants might, using photographs to articulate their feelings of being oppressed, conclude that class and economic oppression is far more important and indeed underpins the other two perspectives. Photovoice therefore does not take a particular account of oppression for granted; rather, the nature of oppression is precisely that which is to be collectively understood with the aid of visual images. Eventually, as the mobilisation turns to political organisation and campaigning—long after the Photovoice project has been completed—the participants may come to modify their understanding of the sources of their oppression.

In the self-development or self-reflection use of Photovoice, individuals in particular situations—such as disability or being on probation—use visual images to reflect on how they ended up in their current situation, the impact on their self-esteem and their view of their life chances and also—though not necessarily—the oppressive penal regime in which they find themselves. The collective discussion of the photographs may indeed result in a shared emphasis on the latter, but there is no guarantee, it might turn—again in a neoliberal culture—into a general collective reflection of the consequences of having made the "wrong choices" in life. Obviously the organisers—if they, for the sake of illustration, are radical penal abolitionists—might attempt to steer the discussion in the direction of structural penal oppression. But this will be just one element in the discussion. Learning this element of their situation will not *define the successful outcome* of the Photovoice project itself.

Education is different: educators know what conclusions they want the students to arrive at out of their discussions. These issues are illustrated in the sociology student project described by Manohar et al. (2014). This was a report on the use of Photovoice in undergraduate sociology teaching in a US higher education institution. The aim was to

> enable students to apply sociological ideas to real-world settings and lived experiences and to theorize the relations of power and privilege as they relate to the structural organization of intersecting categories of difference such as race/ethnicity, class, gender, sexuality, nationality, and age, among others, in which they are positioned.
>
> (Manohar et al. 2013: 37)

This illustrates some important differences of emphasis in the use of Photovoice in the learning and teaching context compared with either those in community mobilisation or self-discovery contexts. The most important is that the theorised description of reality is assumed as given and is indeed already in the possession of the instructors. The role of Photovoice is to get the students to understand this *pre-existing* body of theory rather than arrive at their own conclusions.

The theory in this case takes for granted that social power is a matter of "intersecting categories of difference such as race/ethnicity, class, gender, sexuality, nationality, and age" (Manohar et al. 2013: 37). This is a particular view of social power and stratification. We cannot discuss its validity here but only note that it is taken for granted, while the role of Photovoice is to enable students to understand how these forms of stratification impact on their own personal lives and outlooks. The educational activity is not to critically appraise whether in fact these are the most important forms of social stratification, nor indeed whether they live in a stratified society or a market society of free individuals, as a neoliberal perspective might suggest. In other words, theory comes first and the aim of Photovoice is to help the student understand the theory. The point is again emphasised that the project

> requires students to photograph personally relevant objects or place-based activities around a specific sociological topic, such as gender, race/ethnicity, or work, and then provide a written reflection, *analyzing their photos within learned theoretical paradigms*.
>
> (Manohar et al. 2013: 39; emphasis added)

It is clear that the aim is to get students to interpret their photographs within a theoretical paradigm that is established prior to the activity of Photovoice itself. "Students are asked to take ten photographs documenting the salience of gender in their everyday lives at the micro and macro levels" (Manohar et al. 2013: 40).

Is gender the most salient aspect of your life? The answer has to be yes, otherwise you can't really complete the project. But, coherent with the flavour of most modern sociology there is, of course, a get-out clause: you don't have to come to any particular conclusion. We, the teachers, are not coercing you:

> Students are, reminded that there is no single right or wrong analysis per se, but rather, that multiple meanings can be accorded to a single image, framed by their social location within intersecting axes of domination.
>
> (Manohar et al. 2013: 40)

But this may just compound the problem by coaxing students towards an established account of oppression as always multidimensional. But the various dimensions will still be those, and only those, allowed by the pre-learned theory.

We have, of course, only scratched the surface of the issue here. Indeed much education, especially where the training of practitioners is a focus, can be too easily divided into "theory" and "practice," with only a tenuous relationship between the two. Practitioners in many areas, not only the criminal justice professions such as probation or policing but also social work and community work in general, are familiar with the "I learned the theory" but then when I got out into the "real world," I realised that things were much more complicated and the theory was a very rough guide, if at all. More important was the process of practical learning from more experienced colleagues and going through the process of failing and learning from mistakes. Meanwhile, the theory can always be "rescued" by pointing out that the practitioner has not followed the theory properly or that theory needs to be tweaked to take on board experiences that it failed to anticipate.

A very provisional conclusion might be that the use of Photovoice enables us to start the process of theorisation by allowing theoretical (including political) understanding to emerge out of the critical evaluation of photographs—photographs which have been taken not at random but as the *first stage* of a process of theorising reality (in order to understand and change it).

Photovoice can be used to enable students and practitioners to capture their experiences or the experiences of those they are involved with, prior to learning the theory, and then to enable the latter to emerge precisely as a theorisation *of* the practice. The prisoners and community members discussed above chose visual images and took photographs which reflected a pre-theoretical stage in the formulation of their feelings. The latter were then made more precise through discussion of the chosen photographs. In a similar vein, students and trainee practitioners generally can participate actively in the learning process with images long before they have mastered the more textual elements of scientific discussion, and can allow the latter to develop out of their own discussion of the photographs. They use the theory as a resource to give meaning and substance to their visual images, and use the visual images to give meaning and substance to the theory they are learning. The role of the photographs becomes that of giving a pre-textual, pre-discursive orientation, allowing the latter, as "theory" to ground and clarify itself in dialogue with the image.

Case Studies

The author was involved in a number of case studies using Photovoice with student practitioners in the criminal justice system in three different European countries: UK with Criminal Justice students, Greece with practitioners in probation, and Switzerland with students studying to be social workers/probation officers. Many of the issues discussed above regarding the use of Photovoice in a teaching context were illustrated, and the final part of this chapter will consider these case studies in depth.

In criminology and criminal justice practice, the understanding of social aspects/problems and the various perspectives regarding these issues are one of the main priorities for students to grapple with, particularly in relation to their theoretical understanding. In the case studies below, the students had to learn about the criminal justice system and its different actors, and consider these in relation to the general public's attitudes as well as the situational context of the offenders subject to the CJS interventions. Whilst using the Photovoice method, they had to work out their own views on the wide variety of challenges and current situations in the criminal justice system. At the same time, they were required to examine the differing roles and multiple agencies engaged within criminal justice practice. The learning process was to consider on the one hand reflections on their own perceptions of the criminal justice system and utilise their imagination to convey this, and on the other hand to experience an empathetic process to gain some understanding from other perspectives, for example, those of the prisoners, vulnerable clients, probation or police officers. This brings different lived realities into focus for the students and also at the end introduces these reflections via the final exhibition to visitors, be they other students, academics, interested members of the public and so on. The insights gained through this Photovoice activity elicit deeper and more nuanced perceptions of criminal justice practice and the effects it has on the people subjected to it. By literally viewing the system through a different lens, students themselves create new depictions of the challenges in current situations facing both practitioners and offenders. By engaging in this visceral process, students become active participants rather than passive recipients who are merely engaging with written materials and other depictions of the *researched* person or group (i.e. the probation clients or probation officer).

Case Study 1

In case study 1, the participants were undergraduate criminology students studying a Criminal Justice module at the University of Leicester in the UK. It was the first time that this method was used in criminology education in Leicester. The project was a pilot study and was linked with the second-year undergraduate module "Working in the Criminal Justice System." The project was added to that module and was offered as an additional component for volunteers studying this module. Students had the potential to enhance their grades by including original data from their Photovoice project to illustrate and extend the range within their assignments. By using this new innovative method within the module pedagogy, it was hoped that students would benefit and be able to immerse themselves within the topic, thus engaging with the feelings, challenges and aspirations experienced by practitioners and clients of the criminal justice system.

After explaining the aims of this project via a briefing session to the whole cohort of students, 20 volunteers responded and proceeded with the Photovoice study. The course was organised as six one-hour workshops which took place directly after the core module lecture. During the first session, the students were introduced to theory, practice and ethics of the Photovoice method. Their first task was to go outside their classroom if they chose to and take initial images relating to their expectations and understanding of this new technique. The second session provided students with the opportunity to discuss and reflect on their chosen photovoice images with their fellow students and its potential learning impact. After this second session where students demonstrated their engagement and understanding of the process, they proceeded to the main part of the project, which was to choose to explore a particular aspect of the criminal justice system from both the recipients' and the practitioners' perspective. They were required to research their chosen agency, the theoretical materials relating to their chosen field and then to create a small portfolio of photographs to depict and investigate their agency. The task was how they could symbolise the challenges they had identified and think through ways these challenges could be overcome. During the next few sessions, they brought and shared their images and debated their meanings with the author, as the facilitating teacher interjecting relevant research studies or theories which could explain or enhance their learning, and as Manohar et al. (2013) demonstrated, linking the learning to the wider context. The final two lessons also gave the students the opportunity to be involved in the design of the exhibition poster and discussion of how the final exhibition would be curated and published. The students enjoyed this new dimension of the project, learning about the exhibition process and about art curation, and planning and organising the private view. The exhibition opening took place in the Balcony Gallery of the Attenborough Arts Centre in Leicester. In the exhibition, 15 out of the 20 students involved selected and displayed their work and the gallery exhibited the photographs for a week. Approximately 30 people attended the opening, and the students celebrated their achievements, discussing their images with the audience and receiving live feedback.

The final stage of this project was the assimilation of the photographs within their essays, and there was a clear correlation between improved results and the quality of work, reinforcing the success of this technique in motivating students to explore their chosen agency in more depth and relating this to a higher level of engagement with the theoretical materials.

The students' pictures represented a wide range of different agencies and topics. Most of the pictures symbolised some aspirational dimension such as hope and one's ability to change. Some of these photographs expressed a journey of progress in the context of the prisoner's life or the multiple challenges criminal justice agencies/practitioners have to face within their work. This reflected the students' belief that the system in the UK required urgent and sustained improvement in the way service users were supported to cope with an unknown future and subsequent uncertainty. Other pictures showed the topics of hope and change in a more static manner. Many of the image motifs like landscapes, especially skies and oceans, steep stairs and streets served as symbolic expressions of isolation, alienation and marginalisation of those caught within the criminal justice system. A few expressed hopelessness and a state of total exclusion and futility. Many of the students also reflected on the situation of probation officers in the context of overwork and the enormous challenges confronting their profession. Below are a few examples of the work undertaken by the group with their explanations of the photograph's meaning.

Figure 7.1 *This represents the challenge to the youth justice system of repeat offending and also represents peer influence in offending. (The repeated picture and friends joining. The graffiti represents the low-level crime and their hands behind their back imitates being arrested.)* Taken by Beckii

Figure 7.2 *Way out—The top of the stairs is obscured, so the audience is unsure of the destination, much like when offenders leave prison. Despite being shown the exit, they may never truly be free (as shown by the security camera on the sign, society is always watching them).* Taken by Shannon

Figure 7.3 *CCTV—A prisoner's perspective of the Probation Service. The Probation Service's aims are to prevent reoffending, often through rehabilitative ways. However from a prisoner's perspective, it can sometimes be seen as being constantly watched and observed, more so than in prison. If you want to be released, then you cannot put a foot wrong, it's like having a CCTV camera constantly watching.* Taken by Saunders

Although the students were undergraduates studying criminology for the first time, their images resonated with some of those taken by probation practitioners in Greece and probation/social work students on Master's courses in Switzerland—the other two case studies analysed below.

Figure 7.1 Youth Justice System by Beckii

Figure 7.2 Way Out by Shannon

Case Study 2

In case study 2, a formal lecture for an advance training of probation officers for the Ministry of Justice Defence in Athens, Greece, was presented as an orientation to the project. As above, the Photovoice element was a voluntary opportunity to participate in two extra experiential workshops to find out about and practice Photovoice techniques in relation to probation practitioners' occupational experiences. Approximately half of the original cohort of practitioners volunteered (15 practitioners) to attend to two evening workshops during the duration of their conference with the Greek Ministry of Justice. In the first workshop, the probation officers got a brief introduction to the theoretical background of Photovoice and its purpose without seeing examples of pictures. This was important so that participants felt free to conceptualise and frame their photographs without any influence from previous projects. This was to avoid biases and to let the probation officers identify their own interpretative perceptions. They were then asked to use their smartphones (all participants were happy to use

Figure 7.3 CCTV—A Prisoner's Perspective of the Probation Service by
Saunders

this device) and take pictures in a two-hour slot. Exchanges also took place concerning ethical considerations and expectations. They could opt to walk out and take the shots together in pairs or individually, whichever felt most comfortable and enjoyable. The stress was placed on their creativity, having fun whilst trying to depict their role and the challenges they currently faced within their profession. They were asked to capture how they felt about their job, for example, in terms of both stressful/positive situations and how their clients themselves felt about their situation.

This approach to the workshop had its advantages, especially as there was very limited time available. The participants did feedback that they wished there could have been more time during the fieldwork. For the presentation, which took place during the second evening workshop, each participant had to choose two images for the discussion. The presentations were performed with the help of an overhead projector and two translators. It was interesting to note that some of

Figure 7.4 The Bridge by Nina

the images were very similar to other examples of photographs taken by prisoners/those under supervision in other settings. The feedback was very positive. Not only were the evening sessions enjoyable and informative, but they had also enabled practitioners to share common themes arising from their images. A few of these are illustrated here. Also, some participants could imagine using this method with their clients, particularly to overcome communication barriers. The effectiveness of this idea was discussed within the group, especially when working with younger clients who were more difficult to build a rapport with.

One probation officer spoke of feeling like a bridge between her probationers and the world. She spoke of the bridge being quite daunting in scale, and this symbolised the responsibility and enormity of performing this role for some of the most alienated and vulnerable clients.

This image (Figure 7.5) was of a summer parasol burdened and weighted down by snow (snow is rarely seen in Athens during the winter). This practitioner spoke of her high workload and how at times she was just barely coping, relating this to the umbrella desperately trying to keep upright and function despite being made to carry such a heavy burden of snow.

The images and concerns regarding the work and position of service users was remarkably similar with those studying to become social workers and probation officers at the University of Bern in Switzerland

Figure 7.5 Untitled by Maria

(case study 3). Despite it being a completely different jurisdiction and a cohort of new or nearly qualified staff, the themes resonated with each other, and also reflected an acute awareness of the challenges facing the people subject to probation supervision.

Case Study 3

In case study 3, a two-day workshop took place with ten practitioners undertaking their Applied Masters in social work/probation in Bern, Switzerland. After a very short briefing session to set up the parameters of the project, the students opted to work in pairs. The question they were asked to address by using the Photovoice technique was to think about the role of the probation officers and convey through their images, their perspectives on their job and also how the offenders saw them. In contrast to the project which took place in Greece, the photos were taken on the first day and the theoretical background and input largely took place on the second day. The participants were also given an article to read before the workshop started in order to get a clear impression of the Photovoice method. On the second day of the workshop, the participants had to present their photographs to one another, and later they discussed their results in more depth in groups of three. The results were similar to the other two projects described in this chapter, and

Figure 7.6 Pressure by Ineke

again the pictures produced, communicated powerful messages about the students' experiences and expectations of their forthcoming role.

Some of the themes arising from the Swiss students were confirmation of the challenges faced by practitioners and probation clients across different countries.

This fire hydrant represented to the student who captured the image the sense of an explosive pressure that probation clients can sometimes feel when trying to contain their emotions of fear, anger or a sense of hopelessness. Interestingly, the project undertaken in Germany with those under probation supervision, also had many of these fire hydrant pictures and indicates that this student was only too fully aware of the way her clients felt.

This photograph (Figure 7.7) symbolised the social work student's fear that he would be overwhelmed and overloaded by his role. He felt the image indicated how he would be juggling competing priorities and also how his balance might be affected by the pressures placed on him. His reflections mirrored those expressed by Figure 7.5, taken by

Figure 7.7 Overload by Nils

the practitioner in Greece of the snow-capped umbrella. Photovoice allowed these practitioners to expose their fears and gain a slight distance where it felt safe to discuss their personal reflections on their professions (see Chio and Fandt 2007).

These case studies have reinforced many of the theoretical points raised earlier in the chapter concerning the importance and ability of Photovoice to enhance students and practitioners' self-reflection. The images allow students/practitioners to utilise their insights and experiences to engage with their theoretical learning and recognise the salience of these theories applied to their professional education (Manohar et al. 2013).

Photovoice is clearly a creative learning tool, which as with the earlier examples of research with vulnerable groups of offenders referred to in other chapters, provides a vehicle for self-reflection and self-awareness. These particular skills are essential in these professional contexts and allow practitioners to deepen their relationship with their clients in order to assess their needs more effectively and provide the support and guidance required for desistance and problem-solving.

References

Andreola, B.A. (2006) "Action, knowledge and reality in the educational work of Paulo Freire," *Educational Action Research*, 1(2), pp. 221–234.

Bovill, C. (2020) "Co-creation in learning and teaching: The case for a whole-class approach in higher education," *Higher Education*, 79(6), pp. 1023–1037.

Chio, V.C.M. and Fandt, P.M. (2007) "Photovoice in the diversity classroom: Engagement, voice, and the "Eye/I" of the camera," *Journal of Management Education*, 31(4), pp. 484–504.

Fitzgibbon, D.W. (2007) "Risk analysis and the new practitioner: Myth or reality?" *Punishment and Society*, 9, pp. 87–97.

Freire, P. (1996) *Pedagogy of the Oppressed*. New York: Continuum (Penguin books).

Freire, P. (2005) *Teachers as Cultural Workers: Letters to Those Who Dare Teach*. Expanded edn. Boulder, CO: Westview Press.

Landkammer, N. (2019) *Reengaging Freire: Decoding and Re-Coding Freire's "Generative Images" and Critical Arts Education*. Zurich/Geneva: another-roadmap.net (Intertwining Histories). Available at: https://another-roadmap.net/articles/0003/4709/learning-unit-zürich.pdf (Accessed: 5 January 2020).

Liebenberg, L. (2018) "Thinking critically about Photovoice: Achieving empowerment and social change," *International Journal of Qualitative Methods*, 17(1). doi: https://doi.org/10.1177/1609406918757631

Manohar, N.N. et al. (2013) "Photovoice: A critical pedagogical assignment in the sociology classroom," *Currents in Teaching and Learning*, 5(1–2), pp. 36–51.

Mulder, C. and Dull, A. (2014) "Facilitating self-reflection: The integration of Photovoice in graduate social work education," *Social Work Education*, 33(8), pp. 1017–1036.

Schell, K. et al. (2009) "Photovoice as a teaching tool: Learning by doing with visual methods," *International Journal of Teaching and Learning in Higher Education*, 21(3), pp. 340–352.

Wang, C. and Burris, M.A. (1997) "Photovoice: Concept, methodology, and use for participatory needs assessment," *Health Education & Behavior*, 24(3), pp. 369–387.

8 Audiencing

A Photovoice project requires an audience. This is most obvious in the case of projects aimed at community mobilisation. Where a group of community members have through individual photographs and collective discussion clarified their feelings of how and why their community is oppressed, then there is no point if these insights are not communicated to wider audience. The dissemination of their experiences is part of the process of political mobilisation leading to organisation, media campaigns and so on, and the possible adoption of issues and policies by political parties and pressure groups. In other words, it is clear that there is little point in the initial project unless steps are taken to ensure that the message is communicated to a wider audience.

In the more sober area of individual groups of marginalised people, such as probation clients—or veterans or people with disabilities— reflecting on their situation and their feelings of (for example) the supervision process, then this stage might be thought less crucial. It might be felt sufficient that photography and collective discussion of the meanings and feelings revealed in the photographs is of value in itself. This interactive work serves the purpose of helping the clients survive or make progress in a process of supervision that itself remains unchanged. The research reports or articles arising out of these studies may be able to reflect these experiences to enlighten those interested in the marginalised groups. However, this limits the scope of the projects and returns the power to the researchers, who choose how and where to disclose their findings.

Despite the production of articles or reports emanating from these research findings, this is really to collapse a process of action research into one of individual therapy and subsequent researchers' reflections. Even if the aim of probation clients reflecting on their experience of supervision is not direct political mobilisation, the experience of such reflection is surely one aspect of the process whereby the probation system

DOI: 10.4324/9781003017127-8

learns and develops—in a rational world, criminal justice policymakers would be as much stakeholders as the participants. Thus, in all forms of Photovoice—as action research—the communication of results to a wider audience is a key component.

But the matter does not end here. As we have seen, all Photovoice projects tend to conclude with an exhibition of the photographs, but this is as much for the benefit of the participants—to gain some acknowledgement and take some sort of pride in what they have achieved by giving it a public face. The exhibition as such, however, can easily have an air of celebratory finality to it. This is what we did, these are the photographs we took and which were meaningful to us, and these are the themes which emerged from our discussions: take it or leave it.

But most organisers/researchers—again especially those involved in political mobilisation—will think through the exhibition in terms of a dissemination strategy. The whole political aim of the project may be to get the exhibition to have a mobilising effect on the public and to develop their own interpretative capacity. The audience is to follow in the steps of the original project participants. Thus, the exhibition in such a context serves as a medium for transmitting critical information and knowledge about serious social conditions and issues which can be expected to motivate the audience. For visitors, the exhibition becomes a first-person experience, which can raise fundamental questions about privilege, justice and opportunities, or their absence, in certain parts of community. It can enable the audience to focus on different ways of social support, which can be expressed in productive engagement, critical thinking and personal ways to elevate pain and support desires. These components create a basis for participants enhancing cognitive problem-solving and "bolster motivation, legitimise perspective and realise creativity" (Moxley et al. 2012: 713–714).

This positive attitude to the exhibition can begin to overcome a defect in many Photovoice projects identified by Liebenberg (2018), that is, a failure to pay attention to and document the dissemination process. Such a failure undermines the claim that the Photovoice method can empower and give a voice to marginalised groups (see Chapter 5 for an extended discussion).

But even in more closed contexts, such as probation, where the immediate aim is less political mobilisation than self-clarification, there is an important "audience" of practitioners, policymakers and other stakeholders. For these groups, the results of a Photovoice project involving clients reflecting on their experience of probation might be expected to provoke debate about practical innovation and policy development.

This, of course, is part of a wider theme of "public criminology": of how criminological knowledge (of which Photovoice action research can be seen as one variety) can influence public policy on crime and justice. This is not just a matter of practitioners but also the general public who "need high quality information about the world around them. Nowhere is the gap between perception and evidence greater than in the study of crime and punishment" (Uggen and Inderbitzin 2010: 1). The area of criminal justice, of which the probation system is a major component, is, as far as public perceptions and attitudes are concerned, particularly driven by popular emotions and political calculation rather than by reason and evidence, and this is particularly true in recent decades.

One useful task of public criminology could therefore be that of "evaluating and reframing cultural images of the criminal" (Loader and Sparks 2010: 773).

Of course, if the goal is to create a qualitative and inclusive public discourse on this topic in the face of 24/7 media frequently oriented to the mobilisation of public moods of "righteous anger" about criminal offenders, then public criminology has to focus on a "cooling-down-effect" oriented to the achievement of a stable policy environment including space for reasonable and evidence-orientated decisions. Crimes and criminal justice is a highly politicised topic in society, and this is one main reason why the debates and the knowledge claims are frequently led by "moral panics" (Cohen 2002).

A change towards a more rational orientated treatment of crime is needed. Loader and Sparks demand a "democratic underlaboring" (Loader and Sparks 2010: 776). The public needs to be informed precisely because the development and improvement of the criminal justice system rests so much on public legitimacy. But the process of informing must not be reduced to a simplistic factual or "evidence-based" public policymaking. Such ideology is precisely a recipe for suppressing debate. Rather public discussion must be argumentative, intelligent and serious (Loader and Sparks 2010: 773–779).

How might such a process work in practice? Sanders and Eisler (2014) conducted a public criminology project at Wilfrid Laurier University aimed at public education about criminological topics, using the classroom to bridge the gap between the academy and the public. The problems they faced can be seen as similar to Photovoice projects aiming to communicate their results to a wider public audience.

The Public Criminology project involved a series of seminars, namely ten three-hour classes. The topics were very broad, interdisciplinary and accessible enough to engage the members of the public. Each topic was presented by a keynote speaker. One important component when teaching to transfer knowledge is the ability to "tell good stories" using case stories and using narratives which build upon human interest. Even though the project was successful and the researcher received positive feedback, there were still some notable challenges and scope for improvement. One central issue in any attempt to create a public forum is the difficulty of gaining access to mass media and communication networks. So the dissemination of this particular project remained more local.

It was difficult to measure the impact and outcome of the course. A further difficulty was how to decide where to draw the line between "infotainment" and an academic lecture. Is it more important to satisfy a particular educational standard, or should the focus be more on: getting attention, building up networks and engaging in dialogue by creating a basis, especially in the beginning? The facilitators may decide to increase the academic input as the course progresses. The lecturer has to find a way of reaching the people but still bring in new perspectives, even when this may challenge the way course members think. The knowledge generation and transmission is two way, and thus such a course can bring many opportunities to researchers, course members and teachers. This project certainly created space for new perspectives within policy discussions. One crucial component was to begin to reduce common myths and misconceptions about crime (Sanders and Eisler 2014). This example of a public criminology project shows very clearly how important it is to create a public transfer of knowledge in criminology.

The role of the exhibition in Photovoice is similar: audiencing is precisely what you need, to get an argumentative, intelligent and serious debate going. This is because of the dynamic element in audiencing which distinguishes it from simply that of mounting an exhibition. In something like political mobilisation, you want the exhibition to be a stage in, or contribute to, the mobilisation of large sections of the population—well beyond the original participants in the Photovoice project. The reactions of the audience to the exhibition are thus a crucial new stage—without which the original Photovoice project might fall flat and remain simply an interesting exhibition of photographs which people come and look at and then go home.

Photovoice practitioners have, of course, been aware for some time of the issue of audience impact of the exhibition stage of the project. For example, Robinson (2013) argues that such exhibitions have the potential to be creative and empowering for co-researchers, with the photographs serving as a means for transmitting critical information about social issues, which might otherwise remain unheard, to those in power. Sharing research findings in this way enables researchers to "give back" to co-researchers, stakeholders and communities (Delgado 2015). More generally for visitors, the exhibition offers an immediate and first-hand insight into the social world of marginalised groups. This can raise fundamental questions about privilege, justice and opportunities (Moxley et al. 2012).

Photovoice exhibitions provide a compelling and engaging platform to convey the outcomes of a research project. Providing a space for the display of the photographs, generated during the research study, ensures that a more diverse audience can be reached, and this creates an impact that can move well beyond the traditional academic community (O'Neill 2004). Photographs can also be used to communicate findings to social groups who may not normally engage with conventional research outputs such as journal articles. Whether the exhibition is within a space for a temporary gallery (a large meeting room at the probation centre, as in the case study below) or an established public location like a museum, gallery or studio, the art's infrastructure can provide a means of communication which creates a forum for community discussion and intense personal expression. Interactions with visual imagery encourage audiences and co-researchers to exchange knowledge, personal insights and develop their reflective capacities. This is particularly important when dealing with unconventional and enigmatic problems like offender supervision whose solutions require active engagement from multiple stakeholders (Healy and Fitzgibbon 2019).

The preparation and curation of images for exhibition thus requires careful consideration. The photographs that are presented can influence how audiences "see" and respond to them. To achieve maximum impact, the images must be exhibited in a suitable environment and displayed in a format that is sensitive to the cultural setting, exhibition space and audience (Mitchell 2011).

The role of the exhibition is generally acknowledged to be an active, dynamic process, a stage in the mobilisation of communities or stakeholders. The research methodology of "audiencing" starts from this premise, and by looking at the dynamics of audience reaction to the exhibition seeks to incorporate this reactive process into the research project itself. The aims of most Photovoice projects include wider policy change as a result of giving a voice to people who are usually "done to" rather than "listened to." The purpose of "audiencing" is to investigate whether the relationship between the various stakeholders viewing the exhibition and the original participants in the project has changed and in what ways. For example, will the participants now been taken more seriously, respected for their knowledge and experiences, and have attitudes towards the co-researchers been positively altered?

Audiencing in Action: The Dublin Project

This section of the chapter draws on the research findings from an audiencing project undertaken by Healy and Fitzgibbon (2019) as an extension of their Dublin Photovoice research (Fitzgibbon and Healy 2017). The dynamics of audiencing are illustrated here by using this case study, where the researchers explored the responses from an audience of criminal justice stakeholders to an exhibition of photographs produced by people under probation supervision in Dublin. Ireland is a particularly good place for this sort of research because, as has already been noted in Chapter 6 its penal trajectory is somewhat unique in the Anglophone world. Despite an increasing preoccupation with public protection and risk management, penal discourse in Ireland never truly embraced punitive philosophies or practices (Hamilton 2014). Penal welfare ideals still survive in many parts of the criminal justice system, most notably in probation services where practice requires officers to "advise, assist and befriend" offenders under their supervision. Probation practice is still governed primarily by the Probation of Offenders Act 1907 (Healy 2016). Unlike other jurisdictions, the phenomenon of mass supervision is not so evident in Ireland. The number of people on probation in the community in 2019 was 9,100 (Irish Probation Service 2019) whilst there were 7,170 people in prison (Irish Prison Service 2019). This is evidence of a change in direction as in 2016 there were 11,600 new committals to prison in 2016 (Irish Prison Service 2017) compared to 6,749 supervision orders (Probation Service 2017). So although not so stark as other countries (see Chapter 4) it cannot be claimed that that the country has completely escaped the punitive turn.

The project described here used Photovoice to "make the invisible visible." Probation clients were asked to create a set of visual images to symbolise and portray their supervision experience. The project culminated in an exhibition of selected photographs to showcase the participants' achievements and tell their stories. The exhibition was attended by an invited audience of criminal justice stakeholders. These included policymakers, rehabilitation workers, social workers, probation officers, academics and criminology students. The researchers were interested in evaluating the way the presented images could convey to the audience their intended meanings and the visceral experiences of the co-researchers. By using the technique of "audiencing," the researchers evaluated the exhibition's capacity to influence the audience in terms of their understanding and their ability to learn about the changes and developments that occur during probation supervision.

The Dublin Photovoice project was conducted in May 2016 and involved eight men recruited through a probation-funded, community-based rehabilitation programme that works with adults under probation supervision. The participants took up to ten images and then chose the photographs that were most meaningful to them. They could also provide each with a title or caption if they chose to, but some decided their images should remain untitled. The meanings of the pictures were explored together in focus-group discussions, which were recorded and transcribed. A thematic analysis was then undertaken to identify key themes related to the supervision experience.

The project's artist, Carolyne Kardia, then carefully selected and curated 36 images for the exhibition. She chose images from the ones selected as most meaningful for the participants following focus-group discussions. The exhibition was held in November 2016 at the probation-funded programme where the fieldwork for the audiencing part of the research was conducted. An invited audience of over 30 probation stakeholders attended, and as noted above, these people were mainly involved professionally in the criminal justice system, particularly probation supervision, although some local interested members of the public attended too. The audience was given print-outs of the images with space to write their reflections/impressions against individual photographs. They were asked to record their interpretations and return the sheets once finished. In total, 24 audience members provided written observations. These were then coded and analysed. The first stage was analysis of audience responses to each photograph to gauge the level of consensus and divergence with respect to individual images. After this was completed, audience responses were studied separately from the photographs that had generated their reactions. The observations were coded and grouped into categories in order to identify key themes that emerged across all the responses. Finally, a comparison was made across co-researcher, researcher and audience interpretations to identify and explore the multiplicity of meanings evoked by the images. Ethical considerations were to the fore at all times and the study received ethical approval from the researchers' universities and the Irish Probation Service.

Photovoice researchers such as Delgado (2015) have emphasised that the photographs must be grouped and ordered in ways that are impactful, meaningful and aesthetically appealing. This enables the audience to be guided purposively through the exhibition so that, individually and collectively, the images tell a coherent story. As previously stated, this role was assisted by the presence of an artist as part of the research team who provided invaluable advice about the technical and aesthetic aspects of curating an exhibition. She selected 36 photographs for the exhibition, which were displayed in groups that related to each other. The artist explained her selection as follows:

> The pictures were arranged to metaphorically "speak" to one another, to enable not only the ostensible subject matter to be evident but also the subtle almost unconscious meanings to emerge which are often unintentional. They could be called "mistakes" but somehow convey the complexity of the co-researcher's experience (e.g. the visual structure or composition of a building or wall in a picture may not only convey the recognition and meaning of the place but by its placement in the image also physically shut out the viewer) so the actual tactility of the image is both understood as a narrative but also on a kinaesthetic, or experiential, level too. By emphasising this aspect of the images both for the client and the viewer it allows the process of taking the photograph and subsequently reviewing the image to become a "transformative" experience, allowing the image to re-present itself, depicting previously unrecognised feelings and experiences. The groups of pictures were selected to facilitate and explore these interconnections between subject matter and similar experiences of each of the co-researchers. To use the example of the building, a church may have been taken not only for its place as a retreat and sanctuary, but also an institution with potentially repressive aspects. Each photograph can be interpreted on many different levels and the aim of the curation of the exhibition was to subvert over-simplification of their meanings, to allow their complexity to be exposed and to give the images as well as the co-researchers a voice which adequately reflects this complexity.
>
> (Carolyne Kardia cited in Healy and Fitzgibbon 2019: 8–9)

While this meant that the co-researchers were not involved in the selection process, at least one image from each co-researcher was selected to ensure that all voices were represented. This approach to the curation of the exhibition could be challenged as a reinforcement of researchers' and participants' power inequalities (see Chapter 5 for an in-depth discussion of this issue in relation to the German Supervisible project). The captions or narratives provided by co-researchers were not included, to allow the images to speak for themselves.

Compositional issues such as the size, shape and quality of the photographs can also affect audience responses (Rose 2012). On the artist's advice, images were printed at the highest resolution on A3-size foam-boards, 3mm deep. The images were bled to the edge of the board to maximise their impact and give them greater presence. Foamboard mounts facilitate greater audience engagement. Barriers such as mounts or picture frames could detrimentally effect the viewer engagement with the image. Also, from a purely practical viewpoint, foamboards can be easily hung in a variety of spaces, quickly affixed to walls using Velcro buttons, and removed with minimal damage to the walls or the prints. They are light and durable, which facilitates their use in multiple venues.

At the final stage of any Photovoice project, during image selection and the curation of the exhibition, co-researchers often express anxiety over whether the images they produce are "good enough" (O'Hara and Higgins 2019). Researchers may also have a desire to choose the most accomplished photographs to show their participants' images in the best light, thus choosing not to exhibit images that are blurred, dark or overexposed. In the Dublin exhibition, it was decided that several such images should be exhibited because during focus-group discussions, these so-called mistakes elicited powerful and illuminating responses. Jack, for example, intended to capture a straight-forward self-portrait in the bathroom mirror that demonstrated his transformation from drug addiction to health. On seeing the printed blurred photograph he had actually produced, he immediately concluded, "that's gone wrong" and set it aside. However, the researchers and other co-researchers were struck by the artistic merits of the image. The encouraging discussion on the photograph's merits prompted Jack to explore its personal significance. He explained, "[I wanted] a picture of meself, that looked so well like. From when I went in, there was probably only ten stone left of me like so basically just keeping the appearance of meself, looking after meself." Jack ultimately decided that the photograph was not a "mistake," concluding, "to be honest, I didn't think the pictures would have brought that much out of me. Made me think that much." This example highlights how the amorphous character of photographic "mistakes" can stimulate profound reflection and unlock previously unspoken or unconscious feelings (Healy and Fitzgibbon 2019: 9).

The audience was also struck by this image, and 19 members provided observations on its meaning. A key factor in audiencing was the self-selecting nature of the photographs chosen for comments, so this is a significant proportion of our 24 respondents. The vast majority identified it as "autobiographical" [respondent 21], leading them to speculate on the significance of identity, past, present and future. As one observed, "The man in the mirror. Who am I? Blurring of me, my identity, who I am, what I do" [respondent 18]." Significantly, many detected notes

Figure 8.1 Your Health Is Your Wealth by Jack

of uncertainty and confusion in the image, illustrated by the following statements: "All a blur, not seen for me" [respondent 2] and "looking at life through perspex" [respondent 7]. Obviously, the audience was not aware of his past. Jack had only recently been released from prison. He was therefore experiencing doubts and hesitation with regards to his future. This example illustrates how visual images—including the ones initially viewed as so-called mistakes by the co-researchers—can generate interesting and meaningful, if unintended, synergies between representation and reality.

One of the other areas the researchers wanted to explore in the "audiencing" part of the Dublin project was the notion that visual methods provide a transformative and empowering experience for those involved by enhancing self-awareness and providing the human and social capital needed to engage in social action and advocacy work (Delgado 2015, Wang and Burris 1997). However, if the images and their messages are to enable this to take place, the co-researchers' meaning needs to be effectively communicated to audiences who can effect change, such as policymakers or stakeholders. In order to test this ability of Photovoice to elicit such reactions, the audiencing study explored in depth the extent to which the intended original messages where interpreted and perceived by the target audience; in this case probation policymakers, probation officers, rehabilitation workers, academics and criminology students.

The audience responses to the photographs were almost universally positive and correlated well with the participants' intended messages. Probation supervision was perceived primarily as a source of help and support, a space that fostered creativity and self-expression and provided a refuge from the outside world. For instance, a photograph of the sign at the entrance to the probation centre was perceived to signify "[a] safe place to go to" [respondent 4] and "this probation project which helped me to make positive changes in my life" [respondent 17]. Images of the artwork produced by programme participants received particularly effusive responses, illustrated by the following responses to Jack's photograph of the art-room which generated a total of 16 comments (Figure 8.2): "Creativity. Wonderful. My mess, my space, my expression" [respondent 18], and "colour, chaos and creative, a happy space" [respondent 14]. Just two audience members offered ambiguous views of probation supervision. For instance, one commented, "probation work—payback for past offences" [respondent 16] in response to

Figure 8.2 It's Never Too Late to Learn by Jack

an image of a rubbish bag lying alongside a gardening tool, a statement that has connotations of both redemption and punishment.

These interpretations were largely in line with the meanings that the photographs were intended to convey. Co-researchers expressed overwhelmingly positive attitudes towards supervision within their focus groups, and explained that many of their images represented the help and support they received through their probation programme. They valued the emotional and practical assistance provided by staff and peers as well as the opportunities for growth and education offered by the programme. As Jack, who intended his photograph to represent the transformative potential of art, explained, "it's not basically about art. It's just […] about change, like, learning and change, like to change your life" (Healy and Fitzgibbon 2019: 11).

All these findings suggest that Photovoice methods can be used effectively by marginalised groups to communicate their experiences to stakeholders. The co-researchers who captured the images, were able to communicate to the audience their perceptions of probation supervision as strengths based, welfare oriented and rehabilitative in nature. The audience then mirrored these attitudes towards probation supervision back in their feedback.

Visual methods encourage co-researchers to question preconceived ideas, reflect on personal experiences and engage in intense and emotional dialogues, even around challenging, sensitive or abstract subjects. As Rose (2012: 305) explained, Photovoice inspires co-researchers to "talk about different things, in different ways." Although Rose (2012) was reviewing the impact of Photovoice on image-makers, the audiencing study clearly shows that the Photovoice technique prompted audiences to engage with the lived experiences of the photographers. One audience member reflected that the photographs were "really sombre—gives a great insight into their viewpoint on the community and their place as outsiders within it" [respondent 21]. Certain photographs elicited particularly strong responses, illustrated by audience responses to Figure 8.4, which included: "Brilliant. Crystal maze" [respondent 11] and "I love this but I don't know why" [respondent 8].

The participants and the stakeholder audience could both be described as insiders since they occupied the same penal field, probation, even if from very different positions and power relations. Although their perspectives can bring rich and interesting insights, there is also a potential danger that overfamiliarity with probation mechanisms may obscure novel or unexpected findings by rendering the everyday invisible. Mannay (2010) argues that visual methods can confront this challenge by making the familiar strange and encouraging researchers and co-researchers to reflect on taken-for-granted assumptions by enabling them to gain a distance which encourages fresh and new insights (see also O'Hara and Higgins 2019). The researchers believe that the same may be true for audiences, leading to a new understanding of the supervision experience.

Ultimately, the audience recognised that supervision experiences do not occur in a vacuum but must be considered in light of probationers' relationships with society, including the wider criminal justice system (see also Farrall 2016). Probationers' journeys to, and through, supervision usually involve contact with many criminal justice agents, including police, lawyers, judges and prison officers as well as probation officers. These encounters can shape supervision experiences for better or worse and thus merit further exploration.

Similarly, co-researchers' understandings of supervision transcended its legal boundaries to encompass its wider criminal justice contexts. Like the audience, co-researchers described court appearances and imprisonment in largely negative terms, framing these experiences as "wasted time." This correlates with findings from the English study on women on probation (see Chapter 4). Conversely, lawyers were seen as

Figure 8.3 Help and Freedom by Thomas

advocates and providers of help and support. Although Thomas was not able to attend the focus-group discussion, Daniel, who captured a similar image, commented:

> That's me solicitor's office and me solicitor has got me away with [laughs] too much. He's absolutely brilliant. He usually gets me sent to the hospital or out of charges so he's good. That's why I took a picture of him. And he's done a lot of things for me to change my life around, you know what I mean. He actually got me into treatment before when I was on drugs.
>
> (Healy and Fitzgibbon 2019: 12)

Together, these observations raise interesting questions about the boundary between supervision and its wider social and penal contexts. Most scholars agree that supervision experiences are shaped by people's experiences beyond the probation office (e.g. Farrall 2016, Fitzgibbon et al. 2017). These initial findings suggest that greater attention should be paid to the role of lawyers and other criminal justice professionals in probationers' lives, a topic that is currently underresearched. This example illustrates how Photovoice can prompt audiences (and researchers) to think differently about, and overcome artificially imposed boundaries around, a subject in ways that ultimately expand knowledge and understanding.

Rose (2012: 30) defines "audiencing" as the "process by which an image has its meaning renegotiated, or even rejected, by particular audiences watching in specific circumstances." Meanings are not static but are always dynamically constructed through an interaction between observer and object in particular sociocultural settings at specific times and places (Akerlind, 2012). A range of factors can influence perception, including the image itself, the social setting in which the image is viewed and the observer's life experiences, social identities and cultural assumptions. This was reinforced by the decision to host the exhibition in a local probation setting, which proved highly effective, as the convenient setting ensured high attendance, but also the audience's familiarity with location promoted intense engagement with the images and elicited a sense of empathy with co-researchers' experiences. The audience did not passively absorb the content of images but actively interpreted them through the lens of their cultural and experiential terms of reference. At times this altered the intended meaning. As Spencer (2011: 19) notes, "we 'read' the images in front of our eyes through the pictures we have in our heads." Thus, audiencing studies can be used to shed light on stakeholders' and/or the public's core concerns, values and beliefs.

Analysis showed that audiences actively attributed meaning to images in ways that were shaped by their sociocultural background. For instance, many identified themes in the photographs that called to mind the idea of redemption through suffering. The redemption script is a potent narrative within Western culture which embodies the idea that negative life experiences can ultimately be transformed into positive outcomes (McAdams 2006). This narrative has become deeply embedded into theories of rehabilitation and desistance practices in recent years (Maruna 2001). The presence of this script is best illustrated by the responses to Adam's evocative image of a broken pane of glass lying among weeds which elicited 19 observations from the audience (Figure 8.4), for instance, "shattered lives but green shoots and hope around the corner" [respondent 14], "a shattered life can also be beautiful" [respondent 3], and "hope through difficulty" [respondent 9]. Interestingly, this image was one of the audience's (and researchers') favourites, but was not singled out for comment by the photographer. Significantly the image-maker chose not to give this photograph any caption or title.

The overall alignment between probationer and audience interpretations of the photographs meanings was significant. However, there was

Figure 8.4 Untitled by Adam

Figure 8.5 Relaxing; Time Looking at the Fish by Conor

some divergence in a few cases. These could be explained in part by commonly held cultural assumptions. For instance, Conor captured a close-up of a goldfish bowl that is located in the waiting area of the probation building (Figure 8.5). For him, the fishbowl signified the time and space he could now devote to relaxation and positive thinking due to his participation in the probation project and move away from crime. He vividly recalled his first visit to the programme, explaining, "basically when you come here for the first time, you're asked to sit downstairs while someone comes down to you. You can sit there, sit in the chairs and look at the fish, it's relaxing."

The audience also responded strongly to the image, providing 19 responses in all. In contrast to Conor's intended meaning, the majority identified negative themes in the photograph. For one, the image elicited thoughts of confinement and surveillance: "Colours, vivid. But contained, restricted. No freedom. Only the fishbowl space. The fishbowl of life where I can be watched and monitored" [respondent 18]. Likewise, the comments "Glass cage!" [respondent 10] and "little fish, small pond. Needs more space" [respondent 14] evoke feelings of restriction and confinement. Others spoke of alienation and separation from the surrounding world, evident in the comment, "like a goldfish—on the inside looking out" [respondent 3]. Finally, a sense of futility pervaded some observations, for example, "going round in circles" [respondents 16, 23]. One audience member [respondent 21] even described the photograph as among the "saddest" in the series, seeing in it a representation of the probationer's circumstances. Just four identified positive emotional themes, reflected in the comment "I would love to be like a goldfish in beautiful surroundings" [respondent 19]. This misinterpretation has occurred during other Photovoice projects as well (see Chapter 4) and emphasises the key role the image-makers play in interpretation and reflection.

These examples are interesting in terms of what they reveal about the processes of perception and knowledge production. Images are always interpreted through the lens of shared cultural understandings—a process that sometimes enlightens but at other times misleads audiences as to the intended message. The phrase "living in a goldfish bowl" has a particular cultural resonance that conjures thoughts about a lack of privacy and constant surveillance. However, the image had a different personal meaning for the photographer, reminding him of a quiet, calm and tranquil space. Interestingly, photographers' messages were more easily communicated when the audience and photographer attributed the same meaning to a familiar cultural theme or image, as discussed above in relation to the theme of "redemption." These findings show that audience members are active participants in the interpretation process and are thus worthy of study in their own right. For instance, audience studies could be used to provide insight into stakeholders' core concerns, and to produce a multilayered understanding of the research topic.

The knowledge produced through this process was fluid, dynamic and open-ended, the product of multiple layers of interpretation, created over time as the meaning attached to the images was reflected and refracted through various viewpoints. Each group engaged with the project for different reasons, and their disparate motivations may have shaped their interpretations: the co-researchers wanted to share their experiences of supervision, the researchers to contribute to knowledge about supervision, the artist to set up an attractive and engaging exhibition, and the audience to learn more about probationers' perceptions of supervision. As shown above, the images generated a variety of responses that were sometimes at odds with each other and at other times showed remarkable consistency. Yet, the various perspectives always reverberated through one another. For instance, it is likely that the audiences' interpretations were influenced at least to some extent by the particular groupings and order created by the artist. Likewise, it was clear that observers influenced one another's responses, creating an ongoing conversation about the images as they were viewed (for example, one provided a humorous caption "tyred!!" [respondent 6] for a photograph of a car with a punctured tyre, while another offered a similar but less entertaining "tired" [respondent 7]).

Spencer (2011) contends that the challenges involved in navigating multiple meanings, while complex, should not deter researchers from using visual methods. In our experience, the use of visual methods raises important questions about how to analyse and present data in ways that reflect different ways of seeing.

This section on the Dublin case study has explored audience responses to an exhibition of photographs taken by people under probation supervision in Ireland. The aim was to contribute to the emerging literature on audiencing, an aspect of the Photovoice methodology that is currently underresearched.

Audiencing in the Digital Age

A further issue that could be considered and increase the flexibility and adaptability of Photovoice and audiencing, particularly during the current pandemic/COVID-19 restrictions is the idea of utilising digital platforms to promote and exhibit Photovoice images and also to elicit responses that could in themselves provide useful insights into audience perspectives and perceptions of the subjects being considered. The author has yet to evaluate the potential of the online exhibition, and there may be, of course, special and cultural incongruences that interfere with the accuracy and usefulness of such an approach. However, a virtual exhibition with invited feedback on the photographs could arguably enable the previously invisible or marginalised groups or the relevant community issues to receive wider reach and encourage engagement and improve knowledge. One example of the potential impact of the online exhibition is "Do You See What I See?", found here: https://doyouseewhatisee.narratories.com/index.html (Sethi 2014). This exhibition looks at the relationship between health and employment for refugees from Korea. However, the method could easily be adapted to relate to criminal justice research and criminology.

Conclusion

The discussion and research findings discussed in this chapter suggest that Photovoice methods can be used effectively by marginalised groups to communicate their experiences to stakeholders. Exhibitions of photographic images can help build empathic connections between photographer and audience. Another unique insight indicated that strong practitioner–client relationships can strengthen the sympathetic resonance between image-maker and observer even further. This was demonstrated by a probation worker who correctly guessed which co-researchers had produced which photographs when she was shown the entire set of photographs produced by one of the groups involved in our study in Ireland (four participants). Positive outcomes are not inevitable, however, and depend on the willingness of the target audience to engage with the exhibition and accept constructive criticism (Johnston 2016). While our target audience engaged enthusiastically, other audiences could be less receptive to image-makers' messages.

One of the other less positive aspects regarding the Dublin audiencing study was that none of the image-makers attended the exhibition, either because they had moved on from the programme or preferred to view the exhibition by themselves. There was a five-month delay between the photography session and the exhibition, which the author believes played some part in their decision not to attend. To ensure that co-researchers' voices are represented in the knowledge exchange process, the gap between the photography session and the exhibition is kept to a minimum. It is also key that co-researchers are involved in the planning, curation and hanging of the exhibition, which again necessitates that the exhibition takes place soon after the photographs are taken. This ensures that co-researchers are full members of this important stage of research dissemination.

While this study did not set out to assess change in attitudes towards probationers or probation supervision, studies suggest that viewing Photovoice exhibitions can alter practitioner attitudes in positive ways (see e.g. Flanagan et al. 2016, Fitzgibbon et al. 2017, Fitzgibbon and Stengel 2018). Our findings show that the exhibition encouraged the audience to reflect deeply on the meaning and lived experience of supervision, helping to make the everyday visible and extending their vision beyond the legal borders of supervision. The audience did not passively view the images, but actively interpreted them in ways that were shaped by their cultural and experiential frames of reference, including their occupational background and insider status. As Spencer (2011: 16) notes, "visual representation is always political" because audiences tend to interweave ideological and artistic interpretations. Audience responses suggested a sympathetic understanding of the co-researchers, who were portrayed as people seeking peace and redemption, hopeful but constrained by circumstances that were sometimes beyond their control. Likewise, probation supervision was framed in positive terms as a source of help and support that provided probationers with an opportunity to develop latent talents.

In conclusion, it is widely agreed that visual researchers should analyse the internal narrative of an image as well as its content, that is, the explanation offered by the image-maker. However, this study shows that a full appreciation of visual representations also requires attention to its external narrative, that is, the meanings attributed to imagery by audiences.

References

Akerlind, G. (2012) "Variation and commonality in phenomenographic research methods," *Higher Education Research & Development*, 31(1), pp. 115–127.

Cohen, S. (2002) *Folk Devils and Moral Panics: The Creation of the Mods and Rockers*. Abingdon: Psychology Press.

Delgado, M. (2015) *Urban Youth and Photovoice: Visual Ethnography in Action.* Oxford: OUP.

Farrall S. (2016) "Understanding desistance in an assisted context: Key findings from tracking progress on probation," in Shapland, J., Farrall, S. and Bottoms, A. (eds.) *Global perspectives on desistance: Reviewing what we know and looking to the future*. Abingdon: Routledge, pp. 187–203.

Fitzgibbon, W. and Healy, D. (2017) "Lives and spaces: Photovoice and offender supervision in Ireland and England," *Criminology and Criminal Justice*, 19, pp. 3–25.

Fitzgibbon, W. and Stengel, C. (2018) "Women's voices made visible: Photovoice in visual criminology," *Punishment and Society*, 20(4), pp. 411–431.

Fitzgibbon, W., Graebsch, C. and McNeill, F. (2017) "Pervasive punishment: The shadow of penal supervision," in Brown, M. and Carrabine, E. (eds.) *The Routledge international handbook of visual criminology*. Abingdon: Routledge, pp. 305–319.

Flanagan, E., Buck, T., Gamble, A. et al. (2016) "'Recovery Speaks': A Photovoice intervention to reduce stigma among primary care providers," *Psychiatric Services*, 67(5), pp. 566–569.

Hamilton, C. (2014) "Reconceptualizing penalty: Towards a multidimensional measure of punitiveness," *British Journal of Criminology*, 54(2), pp. 321–343.

Healy, D. (2016) "Desistance, recidivism and reintegration: understanding change and continuity in criminal careers," in Healy, D., Hamilton, C., Daly, Y. et al. (eds.) *Routledge handbook of Irish criminology*. Abingdon: Routledge, pp. 179–196.

Healy, D. and Fitzgibbon, W. (2019) "Different ways of seeing: Exploring audience reactions to images of probation supervision," *Qualitative Social Work*, 19, pp. 663–684.

140 *Audiencing*

Irish Prison Service (2017) *Annual Report 2016*. Dublin: Stationery Office.
Irish Prison Service (2019) *Age and Gender 2007–2019 Prison Committals Report*. Available at: www.irishprisons.ie/information-centre/statistics-information/yearly-statistics/ (Accessed 2 February 2021).
Irish Probation Service (2019) *Monthly Offender Population Report*. Available at: www.probation.ie/EN/PB/0/44D3E689495A08B88025842000428AFD/$File/Web%20Report%20Caseload%20End%20May%202019.pdf accessed 15/2/21
Johnston, G. (2016) "Champions for social change: Photovoice ethics in practice and 'false hopes' for policy and social change," *Global Public Health*, 11(5–6), pp. 799–811.
Liebenberg, L. (2018) "Thinking critically about Photovoice: achieving empowerment and social change," *International Journal of Qualitative Methods*, 17, pp. 1–9.
Loader, I. and Sparks, R. (2010) "What is to be done with public criminology?" *Criminology and Public Policy*, 9(4), pp. 771–781.
Mannay, D. (2010) "Making the familiar strange: Can visual research methods render the familiar setting more perceptible?" *Qualitative Research*, 10(1), pp. 91–111.
Maruna, S. (2001) *Making Good: How Ex-Convicts Reform and Rebuild their Lives*. Washington, DC: American Psychological Association.
McAdams, D. (2006) *The Redemptive Self: Stories Americans Live By*. New York: Oxford University Press.
Mitchell, C. (2011) *Doing Visual Research*. London: SAGE.
Moxley, D.P., Feen-Calligan, H. and Washington, O.G. (2012) "Lessons learned from three projects linking social work, the arts, and humanities," *Social Work Education*, 31(6), pp. 703–723.
O'Hara, L. and Higgins, K. (2019) "Participant photography as a research tool: Ethical issues and practical implementation," *Sociological Methods & Research*, 48(2), pp. 369–399.
O'Neill, M. (2004) "Crime, culture and visual methodologies: Ethno-mimesis as performative praxis" in Ferrell, J., Hayward, K., Morrison, W. et al. (eds.) *Cultural criminology unleashed*. London: Glasshouse Press, pp. 219–230.
Probation Service (2017) *Annual Report 2016*. Dublin: Stationery Office.
Robinson, N. (2013) "Picturing social inclusion: Photography and identity in downtown Eastside Vancouver," *Graduate Journal of Social Science*, 10(2), pp. 20–42.
Rose, G. (2012) *Visual Methodologies: An Introduction to Researching with Visual Materials*. London: SAGE.
Sanders, C.B. and Eisler, L. (2014) "The public would rather watch hockey! The promises and institutional challenges of 'doing'public criminology within the academy," *Radical Criminology*, 4, pp. 37–66.
Sethi, B. (2014) "Intersectional exposures: Exploring the health effect of employment with KAAJAL immigrant/refugee women in Grand Erie through Photovoice," *Theses and Dissertations (Comprehensive)*. 1659. https://scholars.wlu.ca/etd/1659.

Spencer, S. (2011) *Visual Research Methods in the Social Sciences*. Abingdon: Routledge.

Uggen, C. and Inderbitzin, M. (2010) "Public criminologies," *Criminology & Public Policy*, 9(4), pp. 725–749.

Wang, C. and Burris, M-A. (1997) "Photovoice: Concept, methodology, and use for participatory needs assessment," *Health Education and Behavior*, 24(3), pp. 369–387.

9 Concluding Remarks on the Future of Photovoice

This book has been a journey. Like many journeys, it both widens the horizon and at the same time leaves some important places unvisited. We have seen how Photovoice as a research method captures the increasing ubiquity of the visual image as a means of communication and attempts to place it in the hands of those who lack a voice. In other words, Photovoice is part of the attempt to democratise the use of the visual image. The technology makes the photographs easy to take and cheap to reproduce. This of itself is partly democratising, as evidenced by the rise of visual social media. Opening a Facebook or Pinterest account and sharing personal images is cheap in terms of monetary cost and technical knowledge. But as we noted earlier, this process does not necessarily help otherwise powerless people articulate their feelings, either collectively or individually. Indeed, the ubiquity of visual media may, as we noted in the introduction, create an oppressive pressure to conform to self-images dictated by the mass media industry rather than any increase in individual creativity.

The Photovoice project aims to do precisely this: to place the technology in the hands of the voiceless as a starting point for articulating, clarifying and expressing their own feelings and perspectives. Photovoice, as the most radical of the visual research techniques, prioritises co-production and co-researching and equalising the power between researchers and participants, allowing the latter to set the agenda to become the experts and to have a clear voice of their own choosing.

This requires, as we have illustrated in the preceding chapters, a certain attitude by both types of co-researchers, the participants and the organisers. Both need to be prepared to enter into negotiation about the meaning of the visual images which have been created. Where, as in our examples, probation practitioners (or researchers acting in coordination with them) are using Photovoice to enable probation clients to articulate

DOI: 10.4324/9781003017127-9

their experience of supervision, they need to be able to "withhold" judgement, to "withhold" their continual assessment of what takes place to allow the participants to struggle with the issues—through discussing the photographs—and reach their own conclusions. The danger is always that the practitioners and their researchers "already know"—in a broad-brush sense—what the outcome is going to be.

This is particularly problematic in the current climate where research may need rapid and visible results in order to gain funding. By suspending judgement, immersing ourselves in the act of not knowing and actively setting up situations that deliberately enter the 'unknown', we help clients, through detailed interaction with the practitioners, to arrive at a concrete understanding of the experience of probation supervision. In this respect, Photovoice is pushing directly against the tick-box culture which by definition already knows the outcome of the probation experience on clients, and seeks to quantify their responses purely in terms of categories, such as whether their risk profile has changed for better or worse. The use of Photovoice in this context pushes back, in fact, to the older probation traditions of "advise, assist and befriend." Indeed, it pushes beyond them. The old slogan had a strong dose of paternalism, in which the probation officer knows best what is good for the client and what advice to give, from the standpoint of friendship and assistance. Photovoice calls implicitly for the suspending of even this relationship in favour of a genuinely democratic process in which neither the practitioner nor the client knows what the outcome will be until the photographs have been interpreted and discussed. Keeping the research questions open provides the freedom to discover new insights into the research area, such as what supervision really is like for those on probation, for example, how important time, space and place are to those who have been incarcerated or who are on community sentences and therefore experiencing a suspension of their full citizenship.

Practitioners have to be prepared for their expectations about how their clients react to the supervision experience to be shattered by the unanticipated. For example, in Chapter 5, the sense of feeling infantilised by probation supervision was graphically illustrated by the image of a woman leading a child. This was, initially, interpreted by the practitioners as an indication of a caring relationship, but this was completely dispelled by the co-researcher's intended meaning. Thus, the photograph from a Photovoice project provides an experimental, sometimes playful, response that can be open-ended, revealing so many diverse aspects of the client's world.

Our discussion in the preceding chapters, although very much focused on the practical application of Photovoice with probation clients, did venture into some wider discussions and methodological problems. One problem we touched on was the issue of the audience. It is one thing to find a voice through the power of the visual image, and another to have that voice heard and registered such that it has material influence. We focused on Photovoice as a method of enabling marginalised groups of people in institutional settings—we focused on probation clients—to articulate their experiences of the probation process. This is no guarantee that the results will be listened to and understood by probation practitioners.

But in the wider picture we noted, for example, how Photovoice was used as an aid to community mobilisation by helping people articulate their grievances and feelings of oppression in clear ways. The general appeal of Photovoice as a mechanism that can make the invisible visible, that can give a voice to those who are used to being marginalised within society, can be as relevant to deprived communities as it can to probation clients. Indeed, it might be argued that these are ultimately different sides of the same coin. Poor communities find a larger proportion of their young people in prison and on probation. Helping the probation client achieve self-esteem through Photovoice has a parallel with the mobilisation of poor communities to demand resources and political inclusion. Whether we are talking about probation officers or government planners—both can be considered aspects of state governance in the wider sense—the important issue is whether the voices of the marginalised are actually heard. It was for this reason that we attempted to extend the concept of the Photovoice project to include the audience and their reactions to the visual articulations produced by the participants.

It is important, therefore, to understand that there are three distinct groups of people involved in a Photovoice project: the researchers who organise the project; the participants themselves, importantly functioning as co-researchers; and the audience of the general public, hopefully, especially of the practitioners who organise, in our case, probation supervision, and, in the case of community mobilisation, the local and national political elites. In our opinion it is vital to maintain this "holistic" concept of Photovoice rather than just seeing it in terms of the actual dynamics among the participants of taking and discussing photographs, as crucial as these are.

The two levels, of course, are ultimately inseparable. In a general democratic politics with at least some orientation to the classic welfare state ideas of "social citizenship"—the inclusion of all citizens in the basic right to education, minimal living standards and social welfare and care—then the atmosphere will be most conducive to particular institutions like prisons and probation taking seriously the experiences of their particular clients. So the probation centre In Ireland (Chapter 6) and the women's centre in England (Chapter 4) worked particularly well in terms of engagement and positive experiences of those involved because they were located in political systems which (still, despite several decades of neoliberalism) pay general attention to citizens' needs. The interplay between the two levels was, of course, famously characterised by David Garland (2001) as "penal welfare" and, notwithstanding his detailed documentation of its demise in the face of neoliberalism, strong, if patchy elements remain—as we remarked of the Irish probation service—and are very conducive to the productive use of Photovoice.

Each of these three levels of the holistic dynamic of Photovoice presents its own problems. One aspect we highlighted by the use of Photovoice in the teaching context. This illustrated the problem where the teachers already have material that they want to get students to understand and which stretches therefore the notion of the students as co-participants to its limit. But this is to some extent an issue for all forms of Photovoice, and we noted (see Chapter 7) that even the highly democratic pedagogic innovations of Paolo Freire (1996) were not immune from the criticisms that the organisers of projects might have their own agendas, which they wish to silently impose on the participants.

This raises a whole set of issues about who does the research and what are their relations with management. One can imagine a closed loop in which the organisers of the research project take their orientations from practitioners and management and attempt to build these orientations into the structuring of the Photovoice project such that at the stage of discussion, certain themes are stressed rather than others. For example, an emphasis on individual responsibility for criminogenic decisions rather than an understanding of the social and economic conditions which led the clients to find themselves on probation supervision. Indeed, this closed loop might then be reproduced at the audiencing stage where the wider audience of practitioners, managers and policymakers simply find their ideological orientations confirmed as they react to the photographs in the exhibition.

So we made it clear in our focus on "audiencing" that the interactions of the project with the audience (particularly of managers and practitioners) was a crucial part of any project that aimed at having an influence on policymaking and, of course, the "closed loop" scenario is hopefully an exceptional case.

What then is required of organisers and audience to maximise the effectiveness of Photovoice as a holistic process? One of the elements of this that we touched on was the need for digital literacy, and we need to understand this as being as important for the practitioners and managers as it is for the researchers and participant co-researchers. As we said in the introduction, we live in an increasingly visual culture, and this includes everyone, not just people who post images on social media or participate in Photovoice projects. The implication of the successful project which is able to influence policy is a generalised digital and visual literacy. If management can only react to text, speech or at the very most a PowerPoint presentation, then the impact of the Photovoice exhibition will leak away and be diluted. The photographs at the exhibition will appear "interesting" and may even gain a mention in the following day's management team meeting, but only if they illustrate themes already decided upon.

What audiencing involves is something much more akin to Bertolt Brecht's "alienation effect" (1961), by which the famous radical playwright intended to shock his audience away from simply losing itself in the narrative of the drama and turn it into a critical observer of the social issues which lie behind the narrative and the dialogue. In the case of Photovoice it is important, as we stressed, that the audience sees more than simply "nicely put together pictures" and is able to read the personal dramas and the social dynamics behind the particular biographies of the participants in the project

Obviously, in particular focused areas like probation, much more research is needed on what this literacy would look like and how it would enable a more sophisticated reaction to a Photovoice project. We are aware that we have only touched the surface of this. Indeed, a whole series of challenges face researchers and practitioners in engagement via digital platforms.

Although photographs would seem to be an easily adapted method to suit such digital methods as regards engaging participants and enabling their insights to be shared more widely, researchers should proceed with caution. There are numerous ethical issues concerning accessibility– equality of accessibility and also issues such as educational literacy in terms of digital technology and also in terms of the ownership of the images. Being able to ethically work in respect of ensuring confidentiality and consent with regard to the use of the photographs in a public domain needs to be carefully considered. Also, bearing in mind the powerful nature of Photovoice in terms of emotional intensity and the support required when deep-seated trauma or troubling experiences are shared, it would be difficult over digital platforms to provide the support and follow-up necessary to safeguard participants. That is not to say these challenges are insurmountable, but they do deserve very careful consideration and planning. On a positive note, though, all the stories and narratives of the marginalised groups could be more widely disseminated via online exhibitions and hopefully lead to recognition of the challenges facing different communities.

So, finally, where else might Photovoice go from here? Retaining our focus on criminal justice, there are two directions of research. Firstly, Photovoice use as a comparative method. The Photovoice COST programme enabled the comparison of the visual feelings and expressions of probation clients from more than one language community, and therefore overcame barriers of language. This would not necessarily have been possible without this visual form of communication across the communities. Self-expression in terms of images transcends language barriers. This is already part of global culture with the spread of ideographic symbols as in railway stations or airports, which can be read by travellers irrespective of language. In the same way, transnational Photovoice project participants can discuss and reflect on the images taken by people with whom they cannot easily converse in text or speech.

As an aspect of comparative criminology more generally—which has grown in prevalence and popularity over recent years—see Frances Pakes (2019) and Nelken (2011)—one of the strengths of the transcendence of language barriers by Photovoice enables it to potentially play a leading role in comparative criminological studies. This method facilitates the linking of the experiences of different types of marginalised peoples and their relations with criminal justice systems.

A further possible extension is outwards from probation supervision to respond to the needs of people in other areas of criminal justice whose voice is relatively suppressed. There are, just in the criminal justice area, groups of people whose voice is seemingly unheard. Victims of crime, for example, can often be heard only through their lawyers and representatives. Particularly in the case of crimes involving complex relations between victim and offender, as with domestic violence or online abuse, the use of Photovoice techniques in enabling victims to articulate and formulate their feelings would be an invaluable step forward. Indeed, many people who find themselves as prisoners or on probation have themselves been victims—often in childhood. Photovoice could be a way to allow them to explore the results of these experiences in a nurturing and transformative manner. Again, careful ethical considerations would have to be undertaken with appropriate professional support to ensure that victims are not retraumatised by reliving ordeals.

As noted in the early chapters of the book, visual criminology is increasingly gaining traction in social sciences, and new developments linking images with poetry, storytelling and songwriting as well as other more creative options are being attempted in order to promote and understand the lived experiences of those on supervision as well as other marginalised populations (McNeill and Urie 2020, Scott and McNeill 2021).

In a world of increasing complexity, increasing marginalisation and silencing of the powerless of many varieties, and above all a world of increasing dominance of the visual image, as a research method Photovoice has an assured future.

The author found the process of using and perfecting Photovoice as a research technique within the field of criminology enormously rewarding, leading to new insights concerning supervision within the community and the experience of offenders as they try to move towards desistance and full citizenship again. The author would like to thank all those who have participated in the projects contained in this book for sharing their narrative so honestly and with such creative integrity.

References

Brecht, B. (1961) "On Chinese acting." Translated by Eric Bentley. *The Tulane Drama Review*, 6(1), pp. 130–136.

Freire, P. (1996) *Pedagogy of the Oppressed*. New York: Continuum.

Garland D. (2001) *The Culture of Control: Crime and Social Order in Contemporary Society*. Oxford: Oxford University Press.

McNeill, F. and Urie, A. (2020) "Collaboration before collaborative research: The development of 'Distant Voices,'" *Methodological Innovations*, 13(2). doi: https://doi.org/2059799120937270

Nelken, D. (ed.) (2011) *Comparative Criminal Justice and Globalization*. Farnham, Surrey: Ashgate Publishing.

Pakes, F. (2019) *Comparative Criminal Justice*. Abingdon, UK: Routledge.

Scott, J.C. and McNeill, F. (2021) "Sensing supervision through stories and songs". In K. Herrity, B. E. Schmidt, & J. Warr (Eds.), *Sensory penalties: Exploring the senses in spaces of punishment and social control* (pp. 35–52). (Emerald Studies in Culture, Criminal Justice and the Arts). Bingley: Emerald Publishing.

Index

For Product Safety Concerns and Information please contact our EU
representative GPSR@taylorandfrancis.com
Taylor & Francis Verlag GmbH, Kaufingerstraße 24, 80331 München, Germany

www.ingramcontent.com/pod-product-compliance
Lightning Source LLC
Chambersburg PA
CBHW061743270326
41928CB00011B/2353

9 781032 300351